INSIDE MAN

LOYALISTS OF LONG KESH – THE UNTOLD STORY

WILLIAM 'PLUM' SMITH

Dedication

THIS BOOK IS dedicated to my mother, father and family. Also to the thousands of families, men, women and children of Loyalist Prisoners who trekked up every week to the prisons and prison camps undergoing traumatic searches and the rigours of just getting into the prison to visit us. The thousands of supporters who organised and gathered funds to support families while their loved ones were inside the various prisons and prison camps. The thousands of Loyalists who served sentences during a long and turbulent conflict, many who were just teenagers who I often refer to as the lost generation. This is my story, my version but I would encourage other Loyalists to tell their experiences and their stories so that the Loyalist story will not be lost beneath a sea of green.

There are names I mention and incidents I recall but there are many others who I can't name or who I forget in the mists of time but they are all part of this story. Lastly, I would pay tribute to our leader and mentor Gusty Spence and his star pupil David Ervine men who brought Loyalism from the shadows onto a world stage.

This is not a book that glorifies violence but one that brings to the surface the pain, horrors and consequences of conflict and also the resilience of the human race when plunged into adversity.

Published 2014 by Colourpoint Books
an imprint of Colourpoint Creative Ltd
Colourpoint House, Jubilee Business Park
21 Jubilee Road, Newtownards, BT23 4YH
Tel: 028 9182 6339
Fax: 028 9182 1900
E-mail: info@colourpoint.co.uk
Web: www.colourpoint.co.uk

First Edition
First Impression

Designed by April Sky Design, Newtownards
Tel: 028 9182 7195
Web: www.aprilsky.co.uk

Printed by W&G Baird, Antrim

ISBN 978-1-78073-064-6

Front cover: The author photographed within Long Kesh in 1972.
Rear cover: The author posing with a replica weapon within Long Kesh.

Contents

About the Author

WILLIAM SMITH WAS born in Mountjoy Street of the Protestant Shankill Road, Belfast in 1954 into a family of seven. He had a basic childhood upbringing in the poverty that existed in many protestant working class areas. That normal childhood began to change in the 60s as the clouds of civil arrest began to darken the skies over much of Northern Ireland. In the space of 24 hours the relative peace that existed in his world erupted into violence and a cruel, bitter and savage war waged on for over three decades.

The British Army moved into Northern Ireland to separate the fighting factions of Protestant and Catholics, Unionists and Nationalists, Loyalists and Republicans. William Smith, like many of his generation from both communities, became submerged in the bitter street fighting, gun battles, and bomb explosions which teetered on the brink of civil war and brought death, injury and destruction on a national and international scale.

At the age of 17 he was arrested in 1971 for rioting against the British Army and sentenced to six months in Belfast Prison. Upon his release he became re-engaged in the conflict and in July 1972 he was arrested for attempted murder after shooting a Catholic man 14 times. He was consequently sentenced to 10 years and served his sentence in Armagh, Belfast and Long Kesh Prison Camp.

Upon his release he worked in Harland and Wolff Shipyard where he became an active trade unionist fighting for worker's rights. He rose to become a member of the Irish Regional Committee and the UK Power and Engineering Committee. He also campaigned on Human Rights, particularly within the Protestant Community as he believed that Unionist Politicians did not value the Human Rights of Protestants within the conflict.

In 1990, when a window of opportunity opened and shone a light into the darkness of the conflict, he became Chairman of the Progressive Unionist

Party and worked with Gusty Spence, David Irvine, Gary McMichael and Ray Smallwoods in paving the political way forward for a Loyalist Ceasefire along with the Paramilitaries of the Combined Loyalist Military Command (CLMC). He chaired the CLMC Conference in October 1994 that declared the Loyalist Ceasefire. From 1994 to 1998 he was Chairman of the Progressive Unionist Party and was involved in the talks that eventually led to the Belfast 'Good Friday' Agreement.

He has since worked for the Ex-Prisoners Interpretative Centre (EPIC) that represents prisoners from the UVF/RHC constituency, fighting for their rights, Loyalist Conflict Transformation Initiatives (LCTIs) and general welfare issues within the community.

Preface

WILLIAM PLUM SMITH'S record of how he became involved in the so called 'Troubles' in Northern Ireland could be replicated hundreds of times.

Smith's book 'Inside Man' is raw and unvarnished in its telling. We get a graphic picture of learning to adjust to prison life, firstly in Crumlin Road Gaol, later in Armagh Women's gaol and ultimately in Long Kesh.

The characters jump out of this thoughtful book none bigger than UVF man Gusty Spence, a former British soldier who gave focus and direction to Loyalism firstly in prison and later outside of prison.

This publication makes the case for an erudite tome on the life and times of Spence who was a big picture man with a vision. He emerges as the thinker in Loyalism with a roadmap to lead many irascible hot headed young men away from the path of violence. He was a conciliator, always building bridges via the 'Camp Council' designed to obviate clashes between Republicans and Loyalists.

This book highlights the capacity of Spence to mobilise support within the prison administration to win comforts for his fellow prisoners to make their stay in gaol more tolerable. He was behind the cheap black taxi service shuttling families up and down to the Maze from the Shankill and other places.

One of the overwhelming features of Plum Smith's narrative is its honesty. He tells his story simply and clearly. The anecdotes involving individual prisoners and their eccentricities make the book. We hear of 'the mechanic' who casually advises Smith and his fellow prisoners about how he could make guns for them in a few minutes. He availed of metal stanchions which he cut down and then knocked into makeshift weapons. 'Granny McCrea,' a specialist smuggler of goods into the prison delivered the cartridges from which the gunpowder was extracted.

We learn of how necessity time and time again was the mother of invention in terms of weapons training and planned escapes. There is much folklore about Republican escapes especially around people like MLA Gerry Kelly but Plum gives a colourful account of Loyalist escapes from the various gaols... the escape for example, by Thomas Cull.

Smith tells how Loyalist prisoners' lives were run along army lines under the influence of Gusty Spence. Boots had to be polished and regularly buffed. Hygiene and order in and outside of cells were de rigueur. This is not how Loyalism has been portrayed historically.

What comes through again and again in Smith's story is that while war was discussed many, many times Gusty Spence seemed to realise from early on peace was the only way forward. Political options being discussed among the Red Hand Command and the UVF prisoners in 1973 included an 'All Ireland', and the rôle of a Council of Ireland. The term 'Equal Responsibility' instead of the 'Powersharing' was being proposed back then too, all embryos of an arrangement leading ultimately to where Northern Ireland eventually docked politically.

We learn too of secret talks in Cavan involving Deputy First Minister Martin McGuinness, Loyalist Billy Mitchell and other Loyalists who were joined by Seamus Twomey and Daithí Ó Conaill, members of the IRA army council.

A 'no conflict policy' hammered out between Republicans and Loyalists inside the Maze seemed to have worked very well allowing for people like Plum Smith to get a fáinne for speaking Irish having been tutored by Republicans.

What comes across in this book is a comprehensive picture to the effect that the prisoners ran the gaol and if the authorities attempted to act otherwise they met with absolute intransigence and resistance. We gain a bird's eye view through Smith from a Loyalist perspective of the IRA's attempt to burn down the Maze in 1974.

In essence Plum Smith's 'Inside Man' is an important contribution to understanding all of our pasts. You or I could have easily have ended up in Smith's shoes.

Eamonn Mallie

Guide to Terms

2ndIC	Second in Command
Army SLR Rifle	Army Self-Loading Rifle
'B' Specials	Ulster Special Constabulary
CLMC	Combined Loyalist Military Command
CO	Commanding Officer
GOC	General Officer Commanding
IRA	Irish Republican Army
MO	Medical Orderly
MOD	Ministry of Defence
NCO	Non Commissioned Officer
NIO	Northern Ireland Office
OC	Officer Commanding
OIRA	Official Irish Republican Army
OU	Open University
PIRA	Provisional Irish Republican Army
PLO	Palestine Liberation Organization
POA	Prison Officers Association
POW	Prisoner of War
Provos	Provisional Irish Republican Army
PT	Physical Training
PUP	Progressive Unionist Party
RHC	Red Hand Commando
RSM	Regimental Sergeant Major
RUC	Royal Ulster Constabulary
UDA	Ulster Defence Association
UDP	Ulster Democratic Party
UDR	Ulster Defence Regiment
UVF	Ulster Volunteer Force

Selected Events
of the Period

August 1969   Serious rioting began in Derry between Nationalists and police which spread throughout Northern Ireland and quickly became violent. Dozens of houses and businesses were burnt-out, particularly in Belfast. The British Army moved onto the streets at the request of Nationalist politicians and the hierarchy of the Catholic Church, to protect Catholic areas. This marked the beginning of Operation Banner.

October 1969   Publication and endorsement of the Hunt Report recommending the disbandment of the 'B' Specials to be replaced by the RUC Reserve, and that the RUC become an unarmed police force.

December 1969   A split formed in the Irish Republican Army (IRA), creating what was to become the Official IRA (OIRA) and Provisional IRA (PIRA).

July 1970   Curfew imposed on the Falls Road area of Belfast to allow for weapons search, permanently souring relations between the British Army and Nationalist community.

Formation of the Red Hand Commando (RHC).

August 1970   Rubber bullets used by the British Army for the first time.

August 1971   Operation Demetrius (or Internment) was introduced in Northern Ireland.

Long Kesh Detention Centre opened to house internees at the disused Royal Air Force station Long Kesh.

September 1971	Formation of the Ulster Defence Association (UDA).
January 1972	'Bloody Sunday' – 14 people were shot dead by the British Army after a civil rights march in Derry.
March 1972	Northern Ireland's Government and Parliament were dissolved by the British Government and direct rule from Westminster was introduced.
July 1972	Agreement to align RHC and UVF.
	'Bloody Friday' – 11 people killed as over 20 bombs are detonated in Belfast on one day.
	Operation Motorman undertaken by the British Army to reclaim 'no-go' areas in Belfast and Derry.
	Secretary of State, William Whitelaw, introduces Special Category status for prisoners convicted of conflict-related offences.
August 1972	First Loyalists prisoners are moved to Long Kesh.
February 1973	First Internment of protestant prisoners.
June 1973	Northern Ireland Assembly elections held to return members to a new power-sharing Executive.
August 1973	Trials by judge only, without a jury, are introduced after the Diplock Report into legal procedures for terrorist cases.
December 1973	Sunningdale Agreement signed to allow the progression of the new power-sharing Executive.
May 1974	Power-sharing Executive collapses and direct rule is resumed.
July 1974	British Government announces that Internment would be phased out.
October 1974	Much of Long Kesh burnt down by Republican prisoners during organised disorder.
November 1975	British Government announces the end of Special Category status and the introduction of 50% remission on sentences for new prisoners.
December 1975	British Government announces the end of Internment.

March 1976   Opening of HMP Maze (the 'H' Blocks).

October 1976   Prison Officers Association stops all prison visits in response to the murder of another prison officer at his home.

January 1991   Combined Loyalist Military Command (CLMC) announce their formation.

August 1994   IRA Ceasefire.

October 1994   Loyalist (CLMC) Ceasefire.

December 1993   British Prime Minister (John Major) and Irish Taoiseach (Albert Reynolds) issue the Downing Street Declaration.

April 1998   Good Friday Agreement is signed.

Map of Long Kesh

Drawing of the compounds in Phase 5 and 6 made by Loyalist prisoners in 1977.

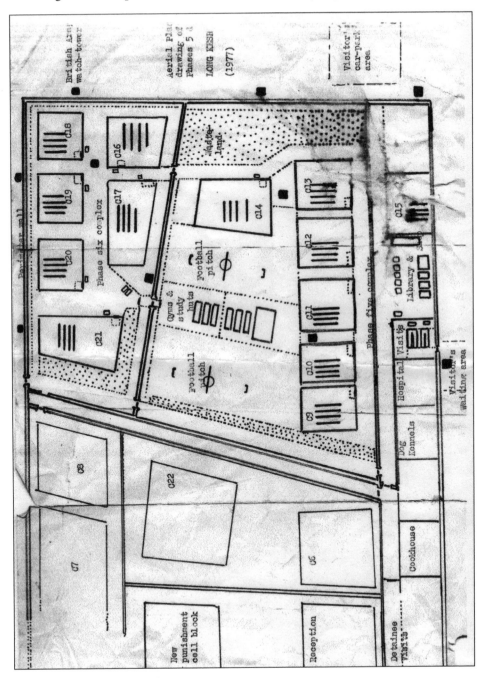

First Word

FORTY YEARS AGO the events in Northern Ireland changed and shaped most if not all of our lives, including mine. At 18 years of age I stood in a courtroom in Belfast charged with the shooting and attempted murder of a catholic man, and I was quickly hoisted on to the conveyor belt system, like some 25,000 other people who passed in and out of prison during the years of the conflict.

My name is William 'Plum' Smith, born and bred on Belfast's Shankill Road, often referred to as "the Heart of the British Empire" even though we owned nothing, sought nothing and got nothing. I was born in Mountjoy Street, named after the famous ship that broke the boom at the siege of Derry in 1688, allowing the Protestants to defeat Catholic King James' army.

This book attempts to explain my prison experience, an experience that took me on a journey from war, to prison, and then to peace. When Loyalism, all of Loyalism, declared its ceasefire in October 1994 amidst the throng of satellite trucks, cameras, microphones notebooks and scribblers, I chaired that conference. My next step was into political negotiations and dialogue that lead to the Good Friday Agreement.

I was in those talks with Gusty Spence, David Ervine, Winston Rea and Dawn Purvis, several of whom, like me, cut their teeth in politics in the compounds and cages of Long Kesh. Much of this is an untold story, and now 40 years after my imprisonment and the bloodiest years of the conflict, I offer this book as another piece of the jigsaw and a contribution to peoples' understanding of how the bomb and bullet was replaced by dialogue and negotiation. This is a Loyalist story, but it is much more than that. In prison we learned by necessity how to talk and negotiate with Republicans, learned we had to share space behind walls, and are still learning how we share this space in freedom today.

CHAPTER 1

The Beginning

I WAS BORN on the 26 January 1954 in the family home at Mountjoy Street on Belfast's Shankill Road. My father Charles William worked in Harland and Wolff Shipyard most of the time. Sometimes he would be paid off on a Friday and onto the boat on a Friday night and off to England or Scotland to seek work in the shipyards there. My mother Isobel stayed at home and raised us in the poverty of a typical working class Belfast family of that time. My two sisters, Margaret and Elizabeth, were followed by me, then my brother Gordon and finally my little sister Jean. Nan, another sister, died at six months of age and I never got to know her.

I loved and cherished going to school and never missed a day. Even during the heavy snowfall of 1963 I trundled through three foot snowdrifts to make it to school only to find that the only other person at school that day was the headmistress who quickly dispatched me back home.

The 60s was an eventful and turbulent decade. In 1961 the Berlin Wall was erected – no one could have foreseen that ten years later after vicious civil strife Belfast would have its own Wall dividing the Protestant Shankill Road from the Catholic Falls Road. The 1962 Cuban missile crisis had everyone glued to a black and white TV, terrified that WWIII was about to erupt with the USA and USSR blowing us all to Kingdom Come and destroying the world with nuclear bombs. In 1963 President Kennedy was assassinated in Dallas and I remember sitting watching this unfold on TV, consumed by the outpour of grief manifested by people in the USA and other parts of the world. The rise of the American Civil Rights movement led by Martin Luther King and the civil unrest and rioting in the USA was overshadowed by the assassination in 1968 of Dr King. The Vietnam War was so unpopular it attracted huge protests all over the world resulting in serious rioting in London, France and the USA, accumulating in young American students being gunned down on the campuses of their own universities by the National Guard. In the heavens the first man landed on the moon. I sat up all night watching this momentous occasion completely enthralled by this expansion into a new frontier. The hippy culture, flower power and the young revolution against authority was manifesting itself in schools, universities, the music industry and other walks of life. I remember getting sent home from school because my hair was too long. The musical revolution with the sounds of the Beatles, Stones, Kinks and many other pop artists was changing the whole world of entertainment. The 60s was truly a revolutionary decade with so many changes and advances happening all over the world.

Meanwhile, back in Ireland, the IRA campaign of 1956–62 was known as the 'Border Campaign' because most of the attacks targeted Police Stations and Customs' posts along the border between Northern Ireland and the Republic. These attacks had petered out due to lack of support, but the spectre of the IRA returning to the stage hung over Northern Ireland like a the Sword of Damocles. In 1965, Sean Lemass, the Irish Prime Minister, met Terence O'Neill, the Northern Ireland Prime Minister in Belfast. This was the first official meeting between two Prime Ministers from these countries. A meeting also took place in Dublin. This political initiative, however small, caused concern among Unionists as many saw it as a step too far and another move towards an All Ireland. Protests and civil unrest followed in the streets and the political temperature began to rise. Although I grew up in the midst of it all, no one could have predicted what the future would bring upon us all.

The IRA blew up Nelson's Pillar in O'Connell Street in 1966 whilst an increasingly restless Protestant population were becoming more frustrated and violent. Various armed groups emerged from within the Protestant community, resorting to causing explosions at the Silent Valley Reservoir, on water pipes, power lines and also becoming involved in assassinations. Demonstrations and counter-demonstrations were occurring on a daily basis, usually ending up street rioting between Protestants and Catholics, and the police. The temperature kept rising and though some people tried to call for calm and restraint, the momentum towards war was unstoppable. I was 15 years old when the balloon went up and the 'Troubles' spread across the country like wild fire. When people ask me now why I ended up becoming involved in the conflict my answer is, "I was born into it".

In August 1969 serious rioting between Nationalists and the police had been going on in Derry for about a fortnight. There was then a decision by Nationalists to spread the resources of the police by expanding the rioting to other areas of Northern Ireland including Belfast. The mainly Protestant Shankill Road, where I lived, ran parallel to the mainly Catholic Falls Road, and the side streets connected both areas like a grid.

On the 13 August a number of homes had been attacked in the Shankill Area, but the attack had been repulsed. Rumours spread that there was to be another attack on the Shankill the next night. I remember going down to Conway Street which ran from the Shankill Road to the Falls Road, with an invisible line somewhere in the middle that separated protestant from catholic. I was with about six friends, all around the same age as me, as crowds began to gather expecting an attack from Nationalists. As the evening approached more crowds from both communities gathered in the streets, facing each other across the roadway. I don't know how it started or who threw the first stone, but at some point the tension exploded into unadulterated violence. Stones then bricks and then petrol bombs flew in the air between the crowds. In a matter of minutes I could see ferocious flames bursting out of homes in the lower Catholic end of Conway Street. People were running from their homes carrying their furniture while others stood and fought in the pitch battles. The violence spread to nearby Cupar Street and Norfolk Street, with pitch battles and petrol bombs again flying through the air as more homes caught fire. There were only a few policemen in the vicinity, who were helpless, and had given up once they had lost control of the streets. Law and order lay with the mobs. Homes and buildings were bursting into flames all over the place and families were running for their lives, carrying whatever possessions they could with them. Then in the midst of this mayhem the first shots rang out and to me it was the point of no return. I knew even at that tender age that things would never be the same.

I walked to home about 500 yards away and you would have thought that everything was normal but for the acrid smell of smoke and the pungent odour of cordite. My mother was at home looking after my younger brother, unaware of the destruction and violence that was erupting a short distance away.

The next day even the news programmes could not capture the ferocity and seriousness of the situation. That morning, I met some of my friends and we headed down to Cupar Street. It was the school holidays and that was where we always hung out. I don't know whether it was the shock and awe of the night before, but I just didn't think I or my friends were in any real danger. There were small groups of people at almost every corner on both sides and the tension and fear gripped the atmosphere as each side stood and stared at each other.

Whether Nationalists felt they were about to be attacked or were just getting ready to defend their area, they were first to blink their eyes, at the junction of Bombay Street and Kashmir Road. A coal lorry was driven across the junction and an armed Nationalist came out of a house with a shot gun. He took up a firing position behind the lorry. Protestants took this as an offensive action and attacked. The gunman behind the lorry opened fire, shooting a Protestant man standing about ten yards from me, hitting him on his neck and shoulders. More Protestants spilled out from the side streets and a full scale riot ensued. More and more Protestants arrived on the scene and petrol bombs began to rain from the sky. Within minutes Bombay Street was up in flames and people were running from their homes. Protestant homes in Cupar Street were also petrol bombed and I remember helping one family get their furniture out of the burning house. As the day wore on barricades were erected by both communities using hijacked cars, buses, trucks and anything that could be used to keep people out or keep people in.

The physical barriers were now in place but people still could not relax nor sleep for fear of the 'other side'. The fear spread all over Belfast and beyond as barricades were erected in the areas that became the interfaces between Protestant and Catholic communities. Groups of men and teenagers appeared on the streets in every area of Belfast, banded together and became known as vigilantes. The British Army moved onto the streets at the request of Nationalist politicians and the hierarchy of the Catholic Church, to protect Catholic areas.

The first sight we got of the British Army was of them coming onto the streets with fixed bayonets, standing with their backs to the Nationalists and pointing their guns at us. The Army then negotiated with communities to have the barricades removed and substituted them with temporary barb wire peace lines. They were confident they would only be in Northern Ireland for three or four months. Four decades later the peace lines have turned to concrete, and the walls are taller, thicker and more plentiful.

The vigilante groups were, however, now more organised and established.

Ironically the first defence association was the Falls Road Defence Association. The vigilante groups then all turned themselves into defence associations. Up sprung the Shankill Defence Association, Woodvale Defence Association, Highfield Defence Association, Suffolk Defence Association and many others. I had just turned 16 and all the young men in the areas were signing up to the defence associations, because after August 1969, people on both sides feared attacks or invasions from each other.

Poignantly the first gun battle between civilians and the security forces broke out on the Loyalist Shankill Road in October 1969. The Hunt Report had been published which recommended that the RUC would be disarmed and the Ulster 'B' Specials would be disbanded. This sent rage and fear throughout the Protestant community. The Shankill Road people massed in their thousands in protest at what they saw as a further appeasement to Republicans and a threat to the whole principles of democracy and an end to the state of Northern Ireland. The fear and rage was so great that rioting broke out between civilians and the Police supported by the British Army. For hours the rioting continued ferociously with running battles between police, soldiers and civilians. I was only 15 at the time and like many young men we felt that we would defend our community no matter who was the aggressor. As the darkness descended soon the petrol bombs began to rain down on the ranks of soldiers and policemen. I remember being chased down a side street by riot squads and the rioters were scattered into the maze of side streets throughout the Shankill. I found myself among about 20 rioters in an enclave of alleyways. The soldiers were further up the side street kneeling down and pointing their guns in the opposite direction. We all emerged from the alleyway and began stoning the soldiers. Then, out of the blue this idiot behind me threw a petrol bomb at a soldier and the soldier swung around and aimed his rifle at me. He had me in his sights. I froze. I didn't want to make any sudden moves in case it spooked him and he shot me. For those few long seconds he had me I thought he was going to shoot me. I thought I was a goner. He then lowered his rifle and I ran like hell. I found the rioter who had thrown the petrol bomb and kicked the shit out of him.

A short time later the first gun shots of the night rang out. It's amazing the way after a few months of conflict it became easy to tell by the noise and sound of a gunshot what type of gun it was fired from. The high velocity British Army issue Self Loading Semi-Automatic Rifle (SLR) had a distinct sound, different from the older bolt action rifles, pistols and revolvers being used by Loyalists. I was back on the main Shankill Road as rioters began to force the Army and Police back down the main Shankill Road. The army had a tactic of every now and then sending groups of soldiers in riot gear, known as 'snatch squads', into the crowd to arrest rioters. A number of men appeared and told us to dive to the ground the next time snatch squads were sent out. We didn't ask why we just did it and the next we heard was a volley of gunshots over our prostrate bodies. It was the last time the snatch squads were used that night as a number of soldiers fell to the ground wounded. The rioters retreated to the corners of the side streets as the gunshots became more frequent. We could hear the distinct shots being fired from the British Army SLR Rifle. From protest to stones to petrol bombs, the violence had now turned into a gun battle.

This man then walked boldly down the Shankill with an overcoat over his arm and I could see the end of a rifle protruding out from the overcoat. I watched in awe as he placed the overcoat on the top of a small telephone pill box raised the rifle cocked it with the bolt and took aim at the ranks of soldiers and police and fired. He fired two more shots then disappeared down a side street with his overcoat over his arm. A few minutes later he appeared and repeated the same action. The rioting was over and the gun battle had begun.

The Head of the British Army, Sir Ian Freeland, had declared that petrol bombers were liable to be shot on sight a few weeks earlier and I knew that soldier who had me in his sights could have shot me dead on the spot. Later that night two protestants from the Shankill Road, Georgie Dickie and Herbie Hawe were shot dead by the British Army for allegedly throwing petrol bombs which was never proven or investigated. They were the first civilians to be shot by the British Army for allegedly throwing petrol bombs. In a cruel twist of fate a protest that began in support of the police produced the first fatality of a member of the RUC. Constable Victor Arbuckle who lived in the area of Lyndhurst at the top of the Shankill was shot dead by a gunman.

In December 1969 the conflict took another definitive twist when the IRA split and the Provisional IRA (PIRA) was formed by Francis Card and William McKee. They lead the breakaway group known as the Provos. The Provos were a sectarian right wing section of the IRA who recruited young men in the Nationalist community who like me were a product of 1969. They were armed initially by the Irish Government who favoured their right wing catholic ethos. One thing was certain the days of vigilantism and protecting Loyalist areas with sticks, stones and petrol bombs were coming to an end and now we were moving towards the vicious, violent and bloodiest chapter in the history of the Irish Question.

CHAPTER 2

From Vigilante to Paramilitary

THE VIOLENCE CONTINUED, riots, protests and shootings became more regular. On the 27 June 1970 I accompanied the Whiterock Orange Parade along Mayo Street with about 30 friends. We were walking on the footpath and when we came to the junction of Mayo Street and Springfield Road, where there was large crowd of Nationalists on the other side of the road. The British Army had allowed them too far up the Springfield Road and when we reached the junction there was a salvo of missiles thrown at the parade and we were all hit and injured. One man, Thomas Reid, was seriously injured and died later in hospital on 3 July 1970. We had no weapons whatsoever, nothing to defend ourselves, so all we could do was to retrieve the missiles thrown at us and throw them back. Eventually, Army reinforcements arrived and they were able to push the Nationalists back down the Springfield Road and the parade was able to continue. However, that was not the last attack as one lodge and band returning from the parade to the Woodvale/Crumlin area was fired upon by IRA gunmen from the Ardoyne area, killing three Protestants, Daniel Loughlins, Alexander Gould and William Kincaid. Another Orange Lodge returning from the parade to East Belfast was also attacked by IRA gunmen, killing a further two Protestants, James McCurrie and Robert Neill. Riots spread in various parts of Belfast and in total six Protestants died from IRA violence and many more were injured. When we had licked our wounds, an inner circle of us got together and swore that never again would we be left in that position of defencelessness. Within days we met in a house and formed the Red Hand Commando (RHC).

We were plunged into almost civil war within a framework of a breakdown in law and order. Most of us were working holding down day jobs and apprenticeships. The Loyalist groupings were still finding their feet trying to form themselves into a competent guerrilla force against the growing and better equipped PIRA. There were no huge arms shipments or gunrunning routes for Loyalists, unlike the PIRA who had initially been supplied weapons from the Irish Government, followed by America and their largest shipment from Colonel Gaddafi and Libya. The PIRA had also set up training camps with the Palestine Liberation Organization (PLO) and some international guerrilla groups of the 70s. They began with American M1 Carbines, American Armalite rifles and then they progressed to the ultimate AK47s topped off with semtex explosives provided by Colonel Gaddafi.

We, as Loyalists, didn't have such impressive connections with the world of armaments. Our first trawl of weapons looked like something from a WWI museum with bolt action Steyr and Torino rifles, shot guns, a few hand guns and very little ammunition. The odd Lee Enfield rifle or Sten sub-machine gun were a luxury but we persevered. If we couldn't smuggle in weapons then we would confiscate the weapons that were already in the country in different hands. Arms raids were carried out on gun shops, private homes and eventually there were a number of successful raids on Army Camps and installations. Explosives were confiscated from quarries and train depots. Soon a considerable number of weapons were accumulated.

However even that caused a problem because we all ended up with different types of weapons. This meant everyone had to be the equivalent of an armourer and we had to learn about the weapons before us, the revolvers, the semi automatics and the fully automatics. The different calibres, .22, .25, .30, .303, .38, .40, .45, almost every type of gun and calibre that was made. Some weapons were made in workshops and factories by semi skilled and skilled workers, such as Zipper guns and copy cat Sten sub-machine guns. Ammunition was also manufactured in factories and workshops. We had bullets with no guns to match and guns with no bullets to match, so among individual Loyalist groupings across the board, bullets were swapped and guns were swapped until we managed to get some type of order among our armoury.

We met in the vacant upstairs room of a public bar where the floor had been layered with old bus seats and there we were trained by an ex-marine commando in the art of unarmed combat, weapons training and guerrilla warfare tactics. We were also taught the skills of interrogation and what to do and how to behave if we were arrested. Once a week we would go to a nearby Baptist Church where we were taught First Aid by the local Pastor. This all occurred against a backdrop of continuing violence that was increasing in venom. Weapon training was going quite well until one night a volunteer was fiddling with an old 32 revolver when it went off accidently. The bullet went through the floor and landed in a pensioner's pint glass in the public bar below.

The Provos were now the dominant faction in the IRA, which led to a number of feuds and deaths within the Republican ranks. More and more soldiers were deployed to Northern Ireland to try to combat the violence. They began to move into both Loyalist and Republican areas, and billeted themselves in police stations, schools and community premises. I lived in Highfield Estate at the time and worked nearby. The army took over premises with the Local Sports Club at Paisley Park. No connection to the Reverend Ian, it was a sports complex owned by the workers of the nearby Mackies engineering firm. They also moved into the Henry Taggart Church, Vere Foster and Blackmountain Primary School. We were regularly rioting with Republicans in the Beechmount and Ballymurphy areas. A new Army Company had moved into the Paisley Park Complex and new legislation was introduced that meant anyone caught rioting was to receive no less than six months imprisonment. In June 1971 we had become embroiled in a riot with Nationalists across the Springfield Road in Beechmount when the British Army based in Paisley Park came round from behind and attacked us from the Highfield Estate. They waded into us with their batons and beat us back into the Highfield Estate while Nationalists cheered from across the road. We all escaped through the alleyways and regrouped in the centre of the Highfield Estate. We were sore and angry and determined to get revenge.

Later on that night we attacked the Army in their billet with stones and bricks for over an hour. Unknown to us they had sent for reinforcements and they trapped us in a cul de sac and I was arrested along with Michael Wright. We were dragged, kicked and beaten the whole way down the street and frog marched down to their billet. We were thrown against the wall and every time a soldier passed us we would get a punch in the kidneys or a baton across the legs. We were classed as juveniles in the eyes of the law, so our parents had to be notified and they had to come for us. Michael like me had never been arrested before. We were taken to Springfield Road Police Station where the police had to wait till our parents came before they could question us. When my parents arrived I told them I didn't want to make any statement and pleaded not guilty. We were both released on our own bail and appeared in court the next week. I pleaded not guilty but was found guilty, however as I wanted to stay in freedom during the summer, I appealed the verdict. I was released on bail and for a few months I was back on the streets. In September I lost my appeal and was sentenced to six months imprisonment. So Michael and I had fallen foul of this new compulsory law even though we had never been in court before. I was a few months older than Michael so he went to Borstal and I went to Adult Prison, on the Crumlin Road. The powers that be had decreed in their wisdom that these tough laws would act as a deterrent. Seven months after my release I was back in prison charged with attempted murder and Michael Wright was killed nine years later by an explosive device which went off prematurely. He was given a full military funeral by his comrades in the UDA.

I headed off to Crumlin Road Prison on my own to face a six months sentence but with good behaviour I would serve only four and be out for Christmas. I hadn't a clue what I was facing at the tender age of 17, but I accepted that I had lost my freedom and would be off the streets until Christmas. I was stripped of all my personal possessions, given an ill fitting prison uniform and locked in solitary for the first day. The next day I was taken to meet the Governor where he read the riot act, all the dos and don'ts, what you were entitled to and what you definitely weren't entitled to. I was then moved to the annex of this adult prison which was known as the Young Prisoner's Centre and allocated to prisoners who were under 21 years old and inside prison for the first time.

I was allocated a single cell which I was to share with another prisoner who was from Downpatrick. I didn't know anyone in the wings. I soon learned that due to rioting in Nationalist areas a few weeks before, there were 108 Catholics and nine Protestants. Of the 108 Catholics, 60 were in for rioting and of the nine Protestants there were only two of us, myself and John McMaster from East Belfast. Ironically we were all in for rioting against the British Army.

My cell mate was a catholic but a decent guy – he hadn't a political bone in his body and just wanted to do his time and get out. The first night in the cell he forewarned me that among the rioters there were a group of Republicans who took delight in beating up Protestants when they came into the wing. Their favourite tactic was to wait until Sunday afternoon when there was a skeleton prison staff on duty and the cell doors were left unlocked between exercise and meal times. That was the opportunity for them to enter your cell and hand out a beating.

The next morning I forewarned McMaster of the situation we were in. We were both assigned to the Wood Yard which entailed chopping wood up all day for fire sticks. It was boring and menial but worse than that we were the only two Protestants out of 30 prisoner's in the Yard. Every other minute were getting bombarded with sticks and when we turned around everyone acted so innocent.

That Sunday after exercise I knew that it was the time that the bully boy Republicans would come to beat me up in my cell. As soon as I entered the cell I grabbed the metal washing can and the metal chamber pot and climbed up unto the top bunk and sat there waiting for them. I heard the cell door bolt being pulled forward so that it wouldn't shut and I jumped up and clenched my only weapons tightly. My cell mate was told to get out and he did – he had no choice but he had given me a chance by forewarning me. In walked McMenamin from the Nationalist New Lodge, I was told he was the bully boy's leader, along with five other prisoners. At first McMenamin tried to talk me down saying that they would get me sometime and I might as well take the beating now. His cronies spread around the bed but I kept my back to the wall and tried to concentrate on the morons around me. I caught a movement to my left and quickly lashed out with the chamber pot and caught one of them right on the head. I then swung the washing can quickly round and the others backed off. McMenamin shouted at me that they would get me and break my legs. They slowly retreated out of my cell but I never dropped my guard until I could hear their footsteps fade into the distance. I sat on the top bunk for an hour until prison officers returned to the wing then I went down to get my dinner. I sat beside McMaster and told him what had happened and to be very wary. I could feel the hatred of their eyes staring at me like daggers sticking in my back.

The next morning when I went down for breakfast McMaster had two black eyes and bruising on his face. I grabbed him and walked him down to the Principal Officers Office and told him we were refusing to work in the Wood Yard due to intimidation. We were both immediately locked up in our cells. We languished in our cells for about an hour until they were opened and a chief officer walked in. He told me I was assigned new duties as an orderly in C Wing. I asked him about McMaster and he told me he was being assigned to the Cook House. I set of to C Wing which ironically housed 300 Republican internees, both Official (OIRA) and Provisional (PIRA) IRA, and they treated me with respect and bore no threat to me. All the orderlies in C Wing were Protestants and none of us were ever threatened or abused in any way. At the weekends the internees would gather and have a sing song where they would sing all the IRA songs and ballads. Being a Protestant I had never heard these songs before but after a few weeks I knew more Republican songs than the average IRA man on the outside.

Everything seemed to be going fine. Remembrance Day was approaching and there was an issue over the wearing poppies. There were four protestant orderlies including me and four Protestants who brought up the dinners every day from the cookhouse and served it to the internees. Concerns were expressed by the Prison Staff about us wearing poppies on the wing on Remembrance Day. However the leaders of both the Provisional and Official IRA internees gave us all assurances that despite the anger and sensitivities of the symbols of what they saw as the British Army, we would be safe and no one would assault or insult us for wearing our poppies. On 11 November we entered the Internee Wing wearing our poppies and began doing our normal work. Although we sensed some tension no-one said anything untoward to us. At dinner time the four orderlies from the cookhouse arrived to serve the dinners. This would be more contentious as each internee would have to queue up and face the four orderlies wearing their poppies to be served their dinner. Some internees refused their dinners and didn't queue rather than be served their dinners. The rest just walked up and took the dinners without making any comments. The first internee to be served was Martin Meehan, a well known Republican and top target for Loyalists. He got served and walked on without saying anything and returned to his cell. Three weeks later on the 2 December he along with two other Republicans, Hugh McCann and Tony 'Dutch' Doherty, escaped from the prison.

Crumlin Road Prison based in the centre of Belfast was amongst the conflict which was manifesting itself on the other side of the wall. We could hear the explosions going off and the shots being fired. At night when we were locked up and a bomb went off or shots fired, the Nationalists would cheer and shout IRA slogans celebrating the death of a policeman, a soldier or anyone who was the victim of the IRA violence. On 29 September a huge bomb went off and they cheered and celebrated as usual. The next morning I learned the bomb had blown up a pub on the Shankill, The Four Step Inn, killing two Protestants, Alexander 'Joker' Andrews, the father of 'Joker' Andrews who I later spent time with in Armagh Prison, and Ernest Bates from the Glencairn area of Belfast.

That morning there were no apologies for the cheering or any two minutes silence. We were just expected to accept that anything the IRA did was legitimate. On 4 December another huge bomb went off near the Prison and the usual cheering, singing and IRA chants followed. The next morning the source of the bombing was revealed as McGurks Bar on the Catholic New Lodge Road, which killed 15 people. The cheers and chants of the night before had dissipated into tears, sadness and anger.

On the day of the funerals, as we sat down for dinner, a Republican prisoner from Downpatrick who I knew was the 'boss' of the Republicans and Nationalists on the wing stood up and brought himself to attention. He then ordered everyone to be up standing for two minutes silence in memory of those who had been killed in McGurks bar. The whole wing of prisoners stood up and when the noise of movement subsided I still remained in my seat. When I looked behind me the other nine Protestants on the wing were also standing. I still remained in my seat. When the two minutes silence was over they all started returning to their cells walking past my table which was under the stairways leading to the landings and I think every prisoner who walked past me spat on me.

I remained in my seat not because I didn't have respect for those killed but because you can't cheer and chant over one death and then expect respect for another. I was reassigned to be an orderly of the Censor's office, which was near the front gate, where I remained for the duration of my sentence. I was due for release on the 26 December but due to it being on a Sunday and Christmas, I was released on the 24 December so I was able to steal three days on the judge, the Prison and the Government which was sweet. Maybe it was my youthful years but the four months seemed to go over my head and I yearned not for freedom but to get back to war as soon as possible.

I left prison on Christmas Eve 1971 and after greeting my family I went to meet up with my comrades. I got an update on the situation and I could see that even in the few short months I was away the war had climbed up to a more serious level. That meant that all organisations were better equipped for war and ready to wage war. We were now uncontrollably heading for a collision course that no one seemed able or willing to stop.

On the 15 July 1972, we made an official mutual agreement with the Ulster Volunteer Force:

The Ulster Volunteer Force/Red Hand Commando Agreement
July 1972

Senior officers of the Red Hand Commando and Officers Brigade Staff sat in discussion of various points relating to the UVF and RHC in July 1972, in which the following points were agreed.

1) Red Hand Commando shall be aligned to the Ulster Volunteer Force and shall work hand in hand in a joint effort to aggregate all resources of both groups and devote their energies to the war with the IRA.

   a) This alignment is taken because;

      1) RHC were in agreement with UVF policy on all matters.

      2) The UVF recognises the right of Red Hand Units to maintain their own separate identity, as a regiment with its own prides and particular style of internal organisation.

      3) It is deemed desirable that both groups become aligned in order to provide assistance and support to each other, politically, physically, financial or materially.

2) Consistent with this agreement, Red Hand shall retain the right to its own command structure of Red Hand Personnel, appointed from within the Red Hand, to legislate and administer to the internal affairs of Red Hand.

   a) Only a Red Hand officer can give an order to Red Hand personnel.

   b) No Red Hand officer can be appointed or "stood down" except from a more senior Red Hand officer.

   c) Wherever UVF policy requires specific action to be taken, the UVF senior officers shall liaise with senior RHC officers in order to have both UVF and RHC working in conjunction with UVF policy.

   d) Wherever it is decided that disciplinary action is to be taken against Red Hand personnel, this must be done by Red Hand officers. However, if UVF officers request that an observer is present during disciplinary action, then so be it. The opposite can also be agreed, allowing an observer from the Red Hand to witness the carrying out of disciplinary action, in specific cases, where an observer would be required.

3) Red hand prisoners shall be housed along with UVF prisoners, under a joint structure of command from senior UVF and RHC officers. Both sets of prisoners shall be regarded as one body of men and will be under the umbrella grouping of the Ulster Volunteer Force. No disagreements between the UVF and RHC outside shall be allowed to effect the good relations and oneness of UVF and RHC prisoners.

4) All members of Red Hand Commando shall be administered the oath of allegiance from the senior Red Hand officer. This oath of allegiance shall be an exact oath, as that taken by UVF personnel, with the exception of three words thus; Red Hand Commando as opposed to Ulster Volunteer Force. No other oath shall be recognised by Red Hand other than that of the adopted UVF oath.

This above agreement was made in Belfast and was established with the will and sanction of representatives of the Red Hand Commando and representatives of the Ulster Volunteer Force.

Signed: Augustus Andrew Spence (Ulster Volunteer Force)

Signed: John Dunlop McKeague (Red Hand Commando)

This agreement was fully honoured later within the Long Kesh camp and RHC officers and UVF officers worked harmoniously for many years facing the hardships of confinement together.

CHAPTER 3

Incarceration

ON FRIDAY 28 July 1972 I stood in the dock of Belfast Magistrates Court, aged 18 years, with my comrade Ronnie McCullough (20 years old), charged with the attempted murder of a Catholic man, Joseph Hall, who we had shot 14 times outside the Catholic enclave of Unity Flats. Our other comrade Tom Reid laid injured in hospital.

We pleaded "not guilty" even though we were caught red-handed. The consequence of my actions did not penetrate the youthfulness of my years. The IRA, Nationalists, Republicans or Catholics were killing people in the Protestant Community and I was retaliating in kind. I had neither sense of remorse, nor a sense of loss of freedom or how long I would lose that precious freedom. I had no regrets, nor did I contemplate what the future would hold.

We were then lead down the steps of the court to the holding cells below where we awaited to transported to prison. I thought we would be going to Crumlin Road Prison not far from my home, but because of the mushrooming prison population and overcrowding there, we were instead to be transported to Armagh Prison. Whilst we waited we were served up the customary two sausages and a chip that, although hard and fusty, satiated my hungry stomach. The clink of locks, keys, footsteps and voices became the sounds that anyone incarcerated would soon become familiar with.

The door opened and police officers entered the cell with two pairs of Victorian handcuffs that had seen better days. We were quickly manacled and escorted to the police van where we climbed the steps of the vehicle to take us to our destination. The events of the past 24 hours had still not fully sunk in as the van door shut and the driver started up the engine. The armoured Land Rovers then positioned themselves and we drove off in a convoy to Armagh Prison, looking out the windows at Freedom Street wondering when we would set foot on those Belfast pavements again.

The journey took about an hour and I sat staring out the windows at the traffic, the green fields, flowers, trees, farmyards and the clear blue sky as we wound our way to the old Victorian prison in Armagh City. The prison wasn't much different than Crumlin Road Prison. It had been used for many functions over the years including an adult male prison, Internment and Borstal. Now however, it was used as a women's prison. The increase in prison population due to the conflict, complicated by the introduction of Internment meant that prisons were overcrowded. Long Kesh Camp, a WWII Aerodrome just outside of Lisburn, had been hastily built to accommodate the overflow and housed internees. Crumlin Road housed non-political, political and prisoners awaiting trial. Remand prisoners just off the streets, like myself were now to be housed in a section of Armagh Prison.

The large gates and Victorian building of Armagh Prison loomed in front of the van and the usual security checks were made before the gates were opened and the convoy entered into the prison yard and headed towards the reception area, where we disembarked with our manacled wrists in front to protect us from falling. One last glance behind me and then we were escorted through the door to undergo the traditional depersonalisation routine upon entry into captivity.

At the reception area we were met by the proverbial prison officer who had obviously wriggled his way into this cushy job. Stripped and searched, we were then directed to a room with four baths with brown stains eroding the enamel and a wooden bung that substituted for a stopper. They appeared as if they were from the Victorian era as well.

There were 90 Republican prisoners on remand who had attacked the eight Loyalists in the prison two weeks before we arrived, and as a consequence, the six Loyalists that remained in the prison had been segregated in a different wing and on an upper landing above those which housed women prisoners. At meal times, Republicans were locked in their cells whist we traversed our landing, through the prison church, got our meal and then returned the same route to our cells to eat our breakfast, dinner or tea. That was okay until 'Joker' Andrews tripped over the church mat one day and semolina and stew were plastered all over the sacred floor.

We were confined to our own landing 24 hours a day and only left it for visits, to see the Governor, the doctor or to see our solicitor. Much of our time was passed away playing cards, chess or draughts which weren't too bad as our cell doors were left open and we could socialise with each other. I was more concerned about my mother having to travel to Armagh to visit me as the welfare section on the outside was only in its embryonic stage and transport to Armagh hadn't yet been factored in.

I got used to the routine pretty quickly and as the days passed away, and in the midst of conflict, I still hadn't thought about what I had done, the consequences of my actions or how long I would remain incarcerated. I didn't contemplate that at 18 years of age my life had changed forever.

CHAPTER 4

First Loyalist feet in Long Kesh

IT WAS A bright summer Sunday on 13 August 1972 and I had just finished my breakfast when a group of prison officers walked in and handed us a black plastic bag each and told us to pack whatever meagre possessions we had. They then searched and led all nine of us out to awaiting prison vans, where they manacled us all before we clambered into the uncomfortable grey transport. We weren't told where we were going, only that we were being moved elsewhere. The prison population was bursting out of control. Sentenced prisoners and those awaiting trial were held in Crumlin Road Prison, Republican internees were held in a new prefabricated prison camp called Long Kesh, so there weren't many options, but we assumed it would be Crumlin Road Prison.

Eighty Republican prisoners were also put into separate vans and then, as the gates opened, we could see a huge security presence of armoured cars and jeeps awaiting us to escort the convoy to wherever we were destined. So, after a few weeks in Armagh Prison, we were on the move to God knows where. The convoy stretched for hundreds of yards as we wound our way through Armagh onto the M1. I'm sure everyone who saw it on that quiet Sunday was wondering what the hell this security mission was all about. Everyone was second guessing where we were going, and Crumlin Road Prison, even though it was bursting at the seams, was the odds on favourite.

We were approaching Lisburn when the convoy turned left off the motorway and unto a narrow winding country road past the Old Blaris Cemetery. To the right hand side construction workers were laying the foundations for what seemed like a new housing estate. That was the first indication we had that we definitely weren't going to Crumlin Road, and the new prefabricated prison camp called Long Kesh captured our imagination. What was it like? Bad stories had emanated from Republican internees about conditions there, so we were wary about what our future incarceration in this new style prison camp would be like.

As we approached the perimeter of the camp, a silvery grey wall of barbed and razor wire, mounted on silvery corrugated sheeting, appeared to stretch for miles. Watch towers manned by armed soldiers and adorned with searchlights made it look exactly like a German Prisoner of War (POW) Camp that one would see in a WWII film. There was no doubt about this place – it was POW Camp. The large double iron gates swung open and the prison vans rolled in just like a wagon train, and we hadn't a clue where we would end up.

The self-contained compounds or cages had four Nissen huts, two wooden huts and were surrounded by razor wire and steel fencing. The van drove down the corridor between the different compounds, and as we looked out we could see that hundreds of Republican internees were standing against the wire looking at this huge convoy and assuming that we were all a new batch of Republicans.

Our van detached itself from the main convoy and we approached an empty compound that had the number seven on it. Prison officers opened the double gates and we entered Compound 7, pulling up at the door of the first Nissen hut. The van doors were opened by prison staff and I was the first to emerge into the sunlight to the cheers of Republican internees. They had gathered in the other compounds to give us a welcome, thinking we were more Republican internees who had been arrested. However, they soon stopped cheering when they discovered that we were the first Loyalist prisoners to arrive in that steel city.

So there we where, nine Loyalist remand prisoners standing diminutively in this big wire cage, four large Nissen huts, a study hut and ablutions all to ourselves and surrounded by seven compounds housing about 500 Republican internees and prisoners. This was the first time 'enemies' could look at each other face to face through steel wire fences. When the novelty wore off we were directed into the nearest hut where we were shown 30 iron prison beds and given blankets and sheets. We paced up and down the hut studying each bed before we selected which one we would occupy. They brought us up food in the prison truck but we had no plates, no knives or forks, no cups and after a number of calls to the prison stores we finally got our eating utensils. All plastic of course!

This was a strange environment for us after being incarcerated in the old style cellular system in Armagh. There was no privacy with nine people all in the same hut. However, after being confined to one landing in Armagh Prison, it was a great relief to be able to walk around the huge compound's yard. The prison staff seemed to make up the rules as they went along. We were told we would be locked up at 9.00 pm every night in the hut until 7.00 am the next morning.

The huge increase in the prison population meant that there wasn't enough prison staff in Northern Ireland. This meant that 90% of the staff in Long Kesh were lured to the prison from England, Scotland and Wales with huge wages and bonuses. They stayed in accommodation in a part of the prison which became known as 'Silver City'. They had their own sleeping quarters, dining room and social bar.

Our first night was very strange as we sat round each other's bed space talking and playing cards. There were nine of us from three different Paramilitary Organisations – RHC, UVF and UDA. There was no command structure, we were all individuals but luckily most of us were from the Shankill area of Belfast and knew each other quite well on the outside. We played cards until the early hours, learning quickly that the lights of the prison shone in through the windows and gave us enough brightness to see. Gradually we retired one by one to our new beds and new surroundings, and drifted off to sleep.

I was awakened at 7.00 am the next morning by the sound of two prison officers turning the keys in the locks and opening the doors. They walked up the centre of the hut counting us in our beds to make sure none of us had escaped! Then they just left without saying a word. Everything was new to us and there was no one showing us how things operated in this barbed wire jungle. Anything we wanted to know we had to go to the gate and ask whatever prison officer was on duty and sometimes even they didn't know.

Eventually our breakfast arrived in a trolley pulled by sentenced criminal prisoners who were used in the cookhouse and for orderly duties. Breakfast was cornflakes, milk and a tea boiler. One of the four huts was designated as a canteen with tables, plastic chairs, plastic knives, plastic forks, plastic mugs, plastic spoons and plastic plates all in abundance, and we sat down and enjoyed a breakfast because we were starving. This again was a strange feeling after being housed in a Victorian cellular prison with its Victorian systems.

It was good having a nice shave and shower instead of washing up in a basin. The next thing was to meet the prison Governor individually to get a run down on the running of the camp rules and regulations etc. I was walked into the Governor's office chaperoned by a prisoner officer on either side to meet the prison Governor, the most ruthless, vindictive and dogmatic man I have ever met. He would have fitted in well at Auschwitz or Sobibór concentration camps. He read the riot act and I could tell we were not going to get much change out of this guy. Everyone who met him that morning was of the same opinion.

We quickly found working with senior prison officers more productive. We started to negotiate for better conditions, reading books, newspapers, playing cards, chess and draught games. Gradually we started to make life inside the camp that little bit better. The food quality was substandard and ironically, because we were remand prisoners on alleged charges, our food was of a lesser quality and had different menus than the Interned prisoners who were classed as less guilty than us. We depended a lot on our weekly food parcels from our families and visitors.

As the days passed our numbers increased as new remand prisoners came in from the streets. 1972 was the most violent period in the conflict and it wasn't long before we were up to double figures, then 20, 25 and 30. The hut was getting crowded so we requested that another of the four huts be opened to ease the overcrowding, which was granted, so we asked for volunteers to move. We began to get more organised and were able to establish a consensus about behaviour within the huts and within the compound. The problem with remand prisoners was the constant shuffling between prisons while awaiting trial. Those released on bail and new prisoners coming in meant it was difficult to have a chain of command. Not to mention that there were three different paramilitary organisations represented among the Loyalist prison population.

Sentenced Loyalist prisoners were housed in the Annex landing of D Wing, Crumlin Road Prison, so we knew that once we were sentenced we would be heading up there. We thought we wouldn't be staying too long in Long Kesh Prison Camp. How wrong that would prove to be! Of course, the opening up of Long Kesh to Loyalist remand prisoners placed a further burden on the organisations on the outside. The prisoner welfare groups within the organisations were already stretched due to the massive increase in the prison population, and now they were spread between Belfast and Lisburn.

Fundraising had to be multiplied to provide prisoners with food parcels and support for their families, and transport was also needed for the prisoners' visitors. A bus was procured and a driver was appointed to ferry visitors from various areas to Long Kesh.

The biggest problem we had in those early days was communication between the inside and outside. The war was still going on and we were eager to hear news from the outside. Letters were censored so our visitors were our only means of proper communication. Being prisoners, soon letters were smuggled in and out during visits but we needed something better. The only prison officers who were from Northern Ireland were high ranking or working on the periphery of the compound's visits and perimeter duties. However, one day a prison officer came to the front door of the hut and shouted my name for a visit. I stopped reading, left my book by bedside and found myself standing face to face with a prison officer who lived a few streets away from me on the Shankill Road. He escorted me to the visiting room about 700 yards away, walking on the road between rows of Republican internees in their compounds. We all soon got used to seeing each other. My visit was over in half an hour and not a second more and we headed back to Compound 7. I had got chatting to this prison officer whom I knew and on the way back I made the approach and asked him to bring a radio in for us, as we were lost for news and needed one with an FM wave on it so that we could listen to police messages as well. He didn't commit himself, however few days later a colleague returned from a visit, escorted by the same prison officer, and walked over to me at my bedside and handed me a radio. We were all delighted.

It was drawing near to our trial and we knew that when we were tried and sentenced we would be transferred to Crumlin Road Prison. We were still pleading not guilty, but we knew we were going to go to prison, it was just a matter of for how long. Monday 4 December 1972 was set out for our trial in Belfast City Commissions. Ninety-five percent of trials in British Courts were plea bargained so we waited for an offer. A few days before our trial we received a visit from our solicitor who told us to "plead guilty and you will receive a ten year sentence and with remission you will be out in six years and eight months". All of us accepted what we thought was a good offer. When we headed for court that day we knew how many years we were getting so there would be no surprises. The judge went through his summing up, and then, as we left the dock, we raised our hands in a clenched fist and shouted "No surrender."

When we arrived at the gates of Crumlin Road we were quite calm as we could now settle in and serve our sentences. Our status had now changed – instead of being remand prisoners awaiting trial we were now fully fledged Sentenced Special Category Prisoners. We were led to the Reception and dehumanised just like Armagh, but we knew we were now heading to the Loyalist Annex at the end of D Wing, where we knew a lot of the prisoners. We were greeted by a welcoming delegation of prisoners, shaking our hands and showing us to our cell. The prisoners ran the wing, not the prison officers who only opened and shut the gates, and escorted us to and from the wings. For about an hour it was bedlam as other prisoners came to our cell to wish us luck and chat to us about things on the outside. Someone brought us a spare radio, fruit, food, almost anything we needed. At 9.00 pm the prison officers entered the wing and everyone retired to their cells for lock up. I was actually glad to hear the cell door shut behind us, as it had been a long day and I was looking forward to relaxing on the bed.

The next morning, at 7.00 am the cell doors were opened and it was slop out time. Chamber pots were emptied and we were given hot water in a basin for a wash and shave before heading down to the ground floor, where we served our own breakfast. The prisoners were well organised, with a chain of command and full control of the wings. They had good communication between inside and outside. The cellular system meant that you could retire to your cell anytime and read a book or listen to your own radio. At night you could be locked up and have all that privacy and maybe write a letter home. The downside was you only got out for certain periods to the exercise yard, whereas in Long Kesh you could walk round the compound all day. The other downside was a chamber pot, whereas in Long Kesh there were two flushing toilets in each hut, and you could go for a shower at any time during the day. However, we settled in to serve our sentences in the warmth of the heated cells in Crumlin Road's Victorian landscape. The quietness was broken quite often in those days by the sound of bombs or gunfire and we would all switch our radios on and listen to the news or police messages.

CHAPTER 5

Escapes (Part 1)

IT WAS A popular misconception that Loyalists did not try to escape and conformed to prison authorities and rules. On 3 October 1972, 21 year old Thomas Cull, who had refused to recognise the Belfast court on the 15 August 1972, escaped from Crumlin Road Prison. The Loyalist wing at that time housed many different Loyalist factions who worked together on all prison issues. A joint escape committee hatched up a simple plan to have one man try to escape. Cecil Lemon, a member of the UDA, was due to be released on the 3 October 1972, having finished his sentence. The committee came up with the cheeky plan of kidnapping Cecil Lemon by overpowering him and tying him up as he showered prior to his release, and then sending another prisoner to go out in his place. It was an audacious plan but a plan that a number of prisoners were willing to volunteer to carry out. Thomas Cull was the prisoner chosen, as he was of the same build as Cecil Lemon.

On his day of release Cecil Lemon entered the washroom to get showered and shaved in preparation for his freedom. He was overpowered by a group of fellow Loyalist prisoners and tied up with intertwined sheets, hidden in the washroom and covered by a blanket. Thomas Cull dressed up in his best clothes, waiting for the prison officer from reception to call to the gates of the wing for "Cecil Lemon's" release. The tension rose in the wing from those who knew what was coming down. Seconds seemed like minutes and minutes like hours but finally the prison officer from the reception area, who would not know individual prisoners, approached the gate and shouted down the wing, "Lemon for Reception". The prison officer in charge on the wing was the one who could throw the spanner in the works as he knew every person on the wing. An officer we called 'Slipper Foot', who because of fallen arches in his feet wore slippers instead of regular prison boots, was on duty, so he needed to be distracted. A member of the escape committee called him over to his cell and complained about repairs and maintenance issues. 'Slipper Foot' fell for the ruse completely and was engrossed in a debate with the prisoner while Thomas Cull slipped out the gates of the wing with a small bag of belongings, just as if he were Cecil Lemon.

However, that was only the first step on the road to freedom. There was a whole release system that Thomas Cull would have to undergo in reception before finally being released. An hour passed without any sign of abnormality in the prison and 'Slipper Foot' shuffled about the wing completely unaware of the prisoner tied up in the washroom. Still the prisoners were unsure if Thomas Cull had pulled off the audacious escape or not but as another half hour passed they were now almost certain that he was on his way to freedom. Then all hell broke loose. A prison officer raised the alarm that Cecil Lemon was lying in the washroom, emergency alarms sounded throughout the prison and prison officers came from everywhere. They rushed into the washroom to find the prisoner lying in a corner, but instead of showing concern for his condition, they marched him straight off to the punishment cells, where he was unceremoniously thrown to the ground and left there.

Immediately, there was a lock down and all prisoners were ordered into their own cells. Having done this, the Wing Officers, who knew every prisoner on their wing, went round each cell to identify who was missing. It was only when they arrived at Thomas Cull's open and empty cell that they discovered who had escaped. Prisoners cheered with delight as 'Slipper Foot' and his compatriots ran about red faced and worried that they were about to become the centre of an inquiry into the escape. Cecil Lemon, meantime, was being interrogated in the punishment cells by senior detectives and Special Branch. He was detained a further three days and then, after a number of protests and representations, he was finally released. A full scale manhunt was launched on the outside, and road blocks and search teams surrounded the Shankill area where Cull was born, but by this time the bird had flown. The boastful record of Crumlin Road being the most secure prison in Great Britain was shattered by a simple, cunning and daring escape plan.

Thomas Cull was rearrested on the 19 July 1974 and charged with "Escaping from lawful custody, contrary to section 26 (A) of the Prison Act (Northern Ireland), 1953".

The following statements were made by the prison officers involved:

Statement of Prison Officer 'A'

I am a Temporary Prison Officer at HM Prison, Crumlin Road, Belfast. On Tuesday morning 3rd October 1972, I was on duty in the Prison and was patrolling the landings on the annex. At about 9.25 am as a result of what I was told, I went to the first floor of the annex and called out the names of two prisoners who were due for release. I called out prisoner 'G' and prisoner Cecil Lemon and two prisoners presented themselves to me. I knew prisoner 'G' by sight but I didn't know Lemon. I asked them to show me their cell cards which they did. They had their property with them and were ready to go out. I took the two prisoners across to the Reception Area where I handed them over to Senior Officer 'B' and returned to my duties. I did not know the prisoner Thomas George Cull by sight.

Statement of Prison Officer 'C'

I am a Prison Officer employed on reception duties at HM Prison, Belfast. On 3rd October 1972 at 9.30 am, two prisoners were passed to me by Senior Officer 'B' for release. They were prisoner 'G' and Cecil Lemon. Each prisoner identified himself to me by his cell card which he had in his possession. I knew 'G' by sight. Each prisoner was given his personnel property, cash etc, Prisoner 'G' was taken to the Governor for completion of his release licence. I then called prisoner Lemon. I had his register card and file before me. His general description answered that on the register. In order to establish his identity I asked him the usual questions, the answers to which are contained in the register card. These questions are – Full Name? Date of Birth? Type of employment prior to committal to prison? Home Address? First name and second name of next of kin? And home address of same? It is not usual to check scars, tattoos etc, and it was not done in this case. There was no photograph of any of the prisoners on file at that time. Having answered all the questions correctly Lemon was released. Prisoner 'G' had not yet returned from the Governor's Office. When Lemon signed his property and cash cards the signatures were similar to those already on the card. I had no reason to believe he was anyone other than prisoner Lemon. A later search of the prison revealed that, in fact, that prisoner Lemon was still inside the prison and that prisoner Thomas George Cull was missing and unlawfully at large.

Statement of Prison Officer 'D'

I am a Prison Officer and employed at HM Prison, Crumlin Road, Belfast. At 7.30 am on 3rd October 1972, I commenced duty on the annex at the Prison. The prisoners 'G' and Lemon are known to me. I knew they were due for release on 3 October 1972. I went for breakfast at 9.00 am and returned at 9.30 am. During that time I was away I was relieved by Prison Officer 'A'. When I returned the numbers book which I inspected was reduced from 53 to 51. I knew that prisoners 'G' and Lemon had been discharged. I carried on with my duties recording the various movements of prisoners. At 11.00 am I walked into the wash-room area for an ordinary routine visit. The wash-room is adjacent to the 'base' or dining room area. To the left of the door in the corner of the wash-room there are two metal rubbish bins. There were also a number of empty rubbish bags. These are large canvas bags used for holding rubbish. I went over and looked at them and saw a person lying behind the rubbish bins. I saw part of his face. I immediately recognised him as the prisoner Cecil Lemon. I immediately went and got Principal Officer 'E' and brought him to the wash-room. I saw Lemon was partially covered with the rubbish bags and hidden from view by the bins. I assisted Principal Officer 'E' to release Lemon . He had his hands tied behind his back with blankets strips. This was cut by me. His hands were swollen and slightly discoloured. A strip of cloth was tied around his head across his mouth to act as a gag. This was cut by me. From the shape of his mouth, it was such that I am satisfied that this was tightly tied. His legs were tied below the knee. When he was released the first thing he asked was to go to the toilet. I had no conversation with Lemon as to how he came to be there. I immediately realised that someone had gone out in his place.

After the escape all prisoners' scars, tattoos, photos and distinguishing marks were recorded in the register card but it was too little too late for Thomas Cull, as the bird had already flown. In September 2012, Thomas Cull and I went back to Crumlin Road prison on a specially organised visit to relive those moments when he walked to freedom. The prison had changed so much since he was last there that he was disorientated and it took him time to collect his thoughts. He told me he was so focused on what he had to remember that he just looked ahead and kept walking, expecting that a prison officer would catch on at any moment. He answered all the questions he had rehearsed and memorised, and even in the interview with the Prison

Governor he thought they would surely realise he wasn't Cecil Lemon, but they didn't. When he walked out the gates of Crumlin Road Prison he was the most surprised person in the world. I asked him who was the other prisoner who was released that day, for the purposes of writing this book, and he looked at me with bewilderment. He said there was only one prisoner being released that morning and there was no one else. Even when I showed him the statements of prison officers he still couldn't remember any other prisoner. He then said to me, "Plum, I was so focused, so concentrated on what I was to do that I was oblivious to anything else around me."

Less than four weeks later, on 27 October 1972, Loyalists would again expose the weaknesses in Crumlin Road when a co-accused of Thomas Cull, 31-year-old James Strutt, escaped. James 'Danny' Strutt had already attempted to escape from another part of the prison while on remand awaiting trial. When he moved to the Loyalist wing, he manoeuvred into the end cell, which had a side window looking on to the Mater Hospital and already had his mind on escaping. In a matter of weeks Danny had smuggled in a few hacksaw blades, which he immediately set to use on the bars of his cell. Danny had noticed that the wall beside the hospital was smaller and had fewer obstacles on the top. His cell mate was also planning to go with him. They cut a cross-part of the bars out over a period of one week, hiding the dust and smearing the cut bars with black polish to look as if they were untouched. Two false heads were created by two other prisoners to conceal the escape. They used carved wood covered in plaster and painted a flesh colour, and even cut their own hair to make wigs.

On Friday the 27 October 1972, the weather was horrendous. With the rain pelting down from the sky, it was a bad night for the security guards but a good night for an escape. James 'Danny' Strutt removed the cut bars from his cell window and then folded his bed over, with the false head placed on the pillow and the wig showing slightly over the blankets. His cell mate did the same with his bed and the two were ready to make their escape. They had made grappling hooks from broken chair legs and ropes from woven strips of bed sheets. Danny was the first to go and he manoeuvred his body through the tight space in the bars before gradually easing himself out onto the road beside the Mater Hospital. His cell mate was next but as he wriggled through the narrow space his thigh caught on a sharpened piece of the cell bars, cutting into his flesh. No matter what he tried to do, he couldn't force himself through without the bar cutting further into his leg. Reluctantly, he withdrew back into his cell and waved to Danny to go on without him before the whole escape fell through. Danny was a good footballer and athlete, so in a matter of seconds he was on top of the wall and dropping himself into the grounds of the hospital. He quickly made his way to the nearby Shankill Road, where he was whisked away to a safe house in another part of Belfast. His cell mate replaced the bars and tidied the cell and bed up. He tightened a bandage made of bed sheets around his leg and lay there till morning.

The next morning the prison officer opened the cell door and counted two prisoners – Jim Irvine and a false head. When he left the landing, the prisoners tidied the cell up, and then went on down the wing for their morning breakfast. Everybody tried to act normal but deep inside they all wanted to give an almighty cheer of elation. It was the second successful escape in 24 days from the prison with such a daunting record throughout the British Isles.

About 10.00 am Principal Officer 'Dolly Grey' entered the wing. He was a former soldier and with his peaked cap over his eyes, he would strut up the wing like a guardsman at Buckingham Palace. He had vast experience and always looked into every cell, spoke to every prisoner and knew everyone by first name. The prisoners knew that if anyone was going to discover that Danny was AWOL, it would be him, so they busied themselves getting extra food, newspapers and other supplies into their cells, knowing from recent experience that another 24 hour lock down would shortly commence. As he approached Danny's cell, everyone held their breath and sure as shooting, he noticed the bars of the cell had been cut and the birdie had flown. His expression was worth a million dollars as he ran out of the cell, hit the emergency bell and shouted, "One off! One off!" Within seconds reinforcements arrived and they were shouting at us to get into our cells for lock up.

Over in B Wing, myself and the other prisoners listened to our radios at newstime as it announced another prisoner had escaped the impregnable fortress of Crumlin Road Prison. We all cheered at the top of our voices, shouting out of windows and cell doors. The political fallout was ringing in the ears and reddening the faces of the prison authorities, as we settled down to a day and night of cellular confinement. However, unlike Republicans, Loyalists on the run were limited to where they could hide. Loyalists could not slip over the border and live a relatively free life in Southern Ireland or stowaway in some ship to the shores of the USA where Irish-Americans would conceal them safely. Instead they were confined to the UK, with sympathisers mainly in Scotland or certain parts of England, and were always under constant fear of arrest. Danny was smuggled across to Scotland, where he joined up with an Operational Unit of the UVF. After about 16 months in half-freedom, Danny was arrested with other members of the UVF while they were raiding the magazine house of a Scottish coalmine for explosives. He was sentenced in Scotland and served a sentence in Barlini before returning to Long Kesh to finish his original sentence.

When Danny returned from Scotland he was charged on 14 July 1974 in Belfast Magistrates Court:

> That he on the 26th or 27th October 1972 at HM Prison, Crumlin Road, Belfast did forcibly break out of a cell within the said prison wherein he was lawfully detained, contrary to section 27 of the Prison Act (Northern Ireland) 1953.

Statement of Prison Officer 'K'

I am employed by HM Prison service as a Prison Officer at HM Prison, Crumlin Road, Belfast, where I am permanent Class Officer in 'D' Wing annex. There are 55 prisoners in this annex, all Special Category Prisoners.

Today, 27th October 1972 I commenced duty at 7.30 am. I was accompanied by Prison Officers 'L' and 'M'. Each officer checked a floor of the annex and counted prisoners. These numbers where returned to me and totalled 55 prisoners, which was correct. At 8.40 am I took the book in which all prisoners names are recorded and carried out a 'head' check. This entails seeing every prisoner and ticking his name of the book. Some prisoners had not left their cells and I therefore had to go round the cell to see these prisoners. I recollect looking in the cell occupied by prisoner James Strutt and seeing what looked like Strutt lying in the bed. At 9.40 am I made another 'head' check and found all prisoners except prisoner James Strutt. I went to his cell and looked at the bed and saw what appeared as someone sleeping as there was a bulge in the bedclothes, but I took a closer look and saw that this bulge was a rolled up blanket with a dummy head placed in the bed. I then reported that prisoner James Strutt was missing to Principle Officer 'N'.

Statement of Prison Officer 'N'

I am a Principle Prison Officer serving in HM Prison Crumlin Road, Belfast.

Today, 27th October, 1972 I commenced duty at 7.30 am in 'D' wing annex. On commencing duty I supervised the handing out of keys to the prison officers on duty in the annex. They then made a body check and confirmed that there were 55 prisoners in the annex. Routine duties were done in the annex until 9.00 am when we were relieved for a tea break. On resuming at 9.30 am I collected keys for the fire exit and about 9.50 am I opened the fire exit door and went out into the enclosed yard. I made a search of this yard and whilst doing so I noticed that the outer bars of one of one of the cell windows had been sawn off. I went inside again and saw Prison Officer 'K' who told me that he could not account for prisoner James Strutt. I realised that the cell window with the bars sawn off was the cell occupied by James Strutt and went immediately into his cell and examined the window. The window was closed and I opened it and examined the inner bars. On touching them a section of these bars fell out. I realised that prisoner James Strutt had escaped from the wing and reported this to Principal Officer 'O'. All prisoners were returned to their own cells and locked in and a thorough check was made. No trace of prisoner James Strutt was found.

Upon his release, Danny worked in Belfast's Harland and Wolff shipyard as a steel erector, where he was unfortunately killed in a tragic industrial accident.

CHAPTER 6

Second time around for Long Kesh

SUNDAY 7 DECEMBER 1972 was our sixth day in the Loyalist annex of Crumlin Road Prison. We retired to our cells for lock up as usual and the prison officers duly came round locking the cell doors and counting us as they went along – just like any other night. I settled down on top of the bed with a book, listening to the radio and the wings began to quieten down. The only noise we could hear was the footsteps of the odd screw, the clinking of keys and shutting of gates. It was nearly midnight and suddenly I could hear all this noise, the opening of gates and many footsteps. Before we knew it the cell door was being unlocked and three British soldiers in riot gear were standing at the doorway. We jumped up from our beds and soon a prison officer walked in with two large plastic bags and a label with a piece of string. He said firmly, "Get dressed, put your personal belongings in the bag and your name on the label – you're moving out". When I looked out onto the landing I could see that the whole place was saturated with British soldiers and prison officers handing out black plastic bags. When I asked where we were going there was no reply.

So here we were again; it was starting to become a habit. We were all herded down the landings and between rows of British soldiers on either side of the ground floor of the wings. At the bottom floor we were processed by prison officers, searched, our belongings were taken from us and we were told they would be transferred separately. The speed of the search meant that almost all of us lost all our contraband, cash, watches and anything else we weren't suppose to have. We were manacled to each other and hustled into awaiting vans. There were about 80 of us and eight vans. It was almost 1.30 am before the vans started moving. Unknown to us, all the Republican Special Category Prisoners housed in 'A' Wing were also in vans and moving in convoy. As we emerged from the prison onto the Crumlin Road, every side street at every junction was sealed off by all types of army vehicles. Down onto Donegal Street it was the same and as we turned into Royal Avenue, while the rest of Belfast slept, the largest convoy since WWII was rumbling through Belfast's city centre. It didn't take me long this time to work out where we were going.

The convoy turned onto the M1 Motorway and rumbled along like a train, with more army vehicles staggered along the road. That night every Army Land Rover, armoured car and soldier in Belfast must have been used in the operation. The M1 had been sealed off to all other traffic so the convoy sped along undisturbed, and shortly after 2.30 am we were entering the silvery-grey barbed wire and fencing that glistened amongst the thousands of lights of Long Kesh camp. We were taken to Compound 12 and as we emerged from the vans, we were taken into the shower cubicles for the ablutions one by one, where we were strip searched and humiliated. The prisoner officers couldn't understand our Special Category Status and when some of us resisted, a riot almost broke out. They then agreed to allow the rest of us to keep our underpants on.

All through that early period in prison Loyalist prisoners had been together, but now they gravitated to their different factions and opted to go into separate huts. I knew then that it was wrong and would only lead to greater problems down the line.

CHAPTER 7

Drill, Discipline and Direction

A CLOUD OF depression mixed with tiredness hovered over the hut as prisoners claimed a bed for themselves. It was less daunting for those of us who had experience of Long Kesh, as we were content to walk around the compound, and the younger prisoners adapted to the situation. However, for the many who had spent a long period in the cellular system in Crumlin Road Prison, it was a devastating culture shock. The open hut system provided no privacy compared to a cell and the six convection heaters offered little warmth, unlike the piped-in heat of the Crumlin. Even those of us who had been in Compound 7 in August felt the low temperatures in the draughty, badly constructed Nissen huts, now that it was December. Many prisoners lay on in their beds with their thin blankets covering them and still wearing their clothes. The only time everyone rose was when their personal belongings arrived and even that was a dampener. Personal items were missing, mixed up and all radios confiscated. Prisoners were angry and when they demanded to see the Governor they were told he was not available. Morale was low.

We were all in the hut looking for our utensils and preparing to get our dinner when the hut doors opened and in walked a figure I knew well, even though his hair had been dyed. It was Gusty. He looked around the hut searching for familiar faces, and most of us were glad to see him. He had been recaptured after four months on the run and held in Musgrave Army Prison Hospital until now.

I had first met Gusty Spence in July 1972. He was being released on parole for his daughter's wedding and the RHC had been asked by senior members in the UVF to provide security, as they wanted his movements known to only a few. The RHC was honoured to be asked and I and my comrade Ronnie McCullough took on the task. We arrived at the pedestrian gate of Crumlin Road Prison at 8.45 am, 15 minutes before Gusty was to be released. We were suited up but the bulges in our inside coat pockets were obvious, and it seemed like ages before we heard the keys turn and the door open. Gusty walked out straight and proud to his first freedom for eight years. We shook hands, greeted him, and walked across the Crumlin Road into the Hammer area of the Shankill to meet some of his family at his brother Billy's home. We stood outside while some of the family had a private moment. The rest of the family were preparing for the wedding. We were his personal bodyguards from the moment he walked out the gates until we ourselves were arrested.

Shortly, a car came and we took Gusty to meet the most senior members of the UVF, including Samuel 'Bo' McClelland and George Orr. The UVF were poorly organised in the Shankill Area and in other parts of the city. In the rural areas there were independent pockets of small groups, also uncoordinated and not very well organised. The leaders of the UVF recognised the leadership qualities of Gusty, his army experience and his iconic status within the Protestant community. They pleaded with him not to return to prison, but while being willing to take on the task, he reminded them all that he had given his word that he would return. We then left to join the wedding preparations. The UVF was desperate to find a way of preventing him from going back to the prison, so that he could assist them in their quest to reform the organisation into a collective fighting force. The next day, as Gusty's nephew Jim Curry drove him back to prison, the car was rammed and armed men descended upon the occupants, assaulted Jim Curry and 'kidnapped' Gusty. We shadowed him as he, Bo McClelland and George Orr went round every county organising the units into viable platoons, companies and battalions that would join a chain of command, as well as organising arms procurements and creating the black taxi companies that would play a vital part in aid and support for prisoners and their families.

Christmas was fast approaching and transport became a huge problem as the prison population continued to grow. Up until then the Orange Cross, formed by Gusty's brother Billy Spence in 1966, was the only formal Loyalist Prisoners' Welfare Association in existence. The formation of The North and West Belfast Taxi Association became invaluable for transport and financial support. Two mini-buses were purchased and departed from designated areas, bringing families to Long Kesh daily.

I had entered Long Kesh in August 1972 as the first and youngest Loyalist, and now I was back just a few months later and there were many more young men like me, with the average age of prisoners having dramatically fallen to below 25. The vast majority of them had never been in prison before. They were raw, just off the street and dumped into this WWII style Prison Camp with open Nissen huts, like dormitories, shared by 30 people, in a wild and desolate place. We looked to our future with apprehension and anxiety.

All the prisoners who watched Gusty walk into the Nissen hut that day looked up to him to lead them and guide them. After the normal greetings and chit chat, he was not found wanting. He called all the officers together within an hour to get an assessment of the situation. At that time, Bruce McMenemy was the second in command after Gusty and had taken over the leadership of the POWs while Gusty was on the run. He promoted Denny Robinson, an old soldier who served with Gusty in the Royal Ulster Rifles, to Regimental Sergeant Major (RSM) and then worked out a plan to raise the morale of the prisoners. Denny, or Danny 'Oh Oh Oh', as we christened him, was the son of 'Buck Alex', a well-known character in Northern Ireland who will always be remembered as the man who kept lions at his terraced house in York Street. He would address all the men the next morning and inform them of his plans. There were whispers and speculation between all the prisoners, but the first order was lights out at midnight, everyone into their beds and go to asleep. Everyone obeyed.

The prison officers routinely opened the hut doors and walked up the centre of the hut to count everyone to make sure none of us had escaped on our first night. This morning it would be different. It was a cold morning but everyone was told to be up at 7.00 am. When the prison officers opened the hut doors we were all standing at the end of our beds. They were startled to say the least. The RSM called us all to attention and Gusty invited the prison officers to count the men. They walked up the length of the hut counting prisoners as they moved along first one side, then the other. Upon finishing their count Gusty asked was everyone accounted for, at which they replied yes, and then they left the hut more quickly than they had entered. The same protocol was performed at 9.00 pm lockup.

It was a subtle way of saying to prison staff that inside the compound we were in control. Eventually, the system evolved to the point where prison staff approached our own hut officers first and requested to take the count in the hut, at which time the officer would call the RSM to have the men stand by their beds and the prison staff would walk up the hut counting the heads.

Afterwards it was off to the canteen for breakfast, then a wash and shave, to 'be on parade' back in the canteen hut where they would be addressed by the Officer Commanding (OC) at 9.00 am. Every person was in the canteen at the appropriate time and formed into columns of three, and were then ordered by the RSM to turn and face the OC, Gusty Spence. He told the men, "You are prisoners of war and you will behave like prisoners of war. You will rise to the highest discipline and cleanliness and remember even though you are in this prisoner of war camp your war in here is just beginning." He explained that the regime would be based on army tradition and together we would survive the rigours and challenges that lay before us. He also explained that he and the other officers would be preparing a routine programme that everyone would adhere to. Everyone would be equal and bully boys would not be allowed to prevail. He also stated he would draw up a list of requests for the Governor to improve conditions in the Camp and asked for cleaning equipment and material to clean up the huts.

Gusty argued that in an open Nissen hut, housing 30 people, we needed to have cleanliness of the highest standard. Every Sunday we would clear the huts of all beds, furniture, lockers etc and everyone would pitch in to scrub every toilet, wash hand basin and shower, and clean and polish the floor. Gusty maintained that personal cleanliness and discipline were necessary so that no one was bullied and the law of the jungle did not rule. Exercise and activities were essential to keep the mind working, for the health of the person and also for morale. We could see the wisdom of his reasoning. Only two people who had served six years in the cellular system of Crumlin Road gave up their Special Category Status and returned to the general prison population. Other than that, everyone else got behind Gusty and supported his leadership to the hilt.

The command structure was based along British Army lines with Gusty as OC, 2ndIC (Second In Command) R McMenemy, RSM (Regimental Sergeant Major) Denny Robinson, and Platoon Sergeant Ronnie McCullough. They were all stalwart supporters of Gusty throughout his own period of incarceration. Gusty recognised Ronnie's leadership on the outside and placed his faith in him that he could put those qualities to use inside Long Kesh.

1972 had seen the worst year of violence and we were now into 1973 with the same expectation of another violent year. There was very little to do. We were kept busy in the morning as Gusty drew up a regime to boost morale, health, discipline and cleanliness. It went something like this (see Appendix 1):

8.30 am	Reveille
9.00 am	PE
10.00 am	Muster Parade and Inspection
10.15 am	Hut and Bed Inspection
10.30 am	Drill Training and Exercise
Afternoon	Bomb Making Classes
	Weapons Training
	Guerrilla Tactics

The afternoons were occupied doing classes in connection with the war outside. There was nothing available from the prison authorities by way of education, so Long Kesh soon got the title of 'University of Terrorism'. We even made facsimiles of weapons from wood, chair legs, plastic and anything else we could get our hands on. Some of them were very realistic and we would use them in weapons training classes.

Gusty requested to see the prison Governor or senior prison officer to negotiate some concessions from the authorities. Simple things that could so mean much to the men behind the wire fortress, like a radio, tea boiler, access to the Prison Shop, newspapers, writing paper, and books. He also got the men to fill out a list of missing or damaged personal belongings incurred on the transfer from Belfast's Crumlin Prison. The Governor, refused to recognise any type of command structure; as far as he was concerned we were all criminals and he was the only Kommandant in the camp. Senior prison officers, who were all from Northern Ireland and had moved from Crumlin Road Prison, knew the culture better and acknowledged the need for some type of structure to communicate with the prison population, and they met with Gusty. Family visits, legal visits, letters, cleaning materials, a list of damaged and missing belongings were all given to senior prison officers.

We received a few of the requests like cleaning materials, and one A4 page to write letters. Other than that, family visiting was in chaos and the Governor still refused to meet our representative. Men were becoming angry and impatient but in this prison camp the British Army was always on standby for riot duty.

Not to be outdone, we came up with a wonderful peaceful line of attack using the prison rules as a weapon. All prisoners had the right to request to see a Governor or Assistant Governor, the doctor, the welfare, the dentist, and a religious minister every day if they so wished. Every morning prison officers would enter the huts and ask prisoners if they would like to make any requests. Every one of us to a man requested to see the Governor, the doctor, the welfare, the dentist and a minister. Needless to say this brought the whole administration in the prison to a halt. It lasted for two days until the prison authorities relented. They agreed that we could have a representative meet with an Assistant Governor; the Governor still refused, but we felt we had achieved enough for the present. Our own officers went round to each prisoner listing all requests and gave them to Gusty. The next morning the Assistant Governor arrived at the prison officer's hut and Gusty went out to meet him. He produced the list and told the Governor that in the future we could do the requests ourselves and work out a fairer system for rotation of visits, thus slowly siphoning control from the authorities and placing at least part of our destiny in our own hands.

The morale had been boosted, discipline had been implanted, so now we turned to the war within the camp. The struggle for more humane conditions and the battle of minds had begun.

Danny 'Oh, Oh, Oh' had served in the army with Gusty and they had done their army training in a boot camp in England. The huts in boot camp were very similar to those in Long Kesh so they had decided to run the prison camp along similar lines. We were the raw recruits and none of us had done any drill or marching, except the basic principles in the streets. Every morning, every able bodied prisoner was assembled in the compound, which became our parade ground, and in columns of three we would set off and complete ten laps, and then there would be 30 minutes of physical exercise. Danny was snapping at our heels every minute, making sure everyone did their exercise and there were no malingerers. At first he really used to get to us but we grew to respect him, as he did every lap and every exercise, and he treated everyone the same. Within a short time we would do anything for him.

After physical training (PT) it was in for a shower and shave, make your 'bed pack' British Army style, clean around your bed space and have your footwear polished. Then it was back on the 'parade ground' for 10.00 am Muster Parade. The Commanding Officer (CO) would inspect the ranks to make sure everyone was clean and tidy. After inspection it was time to retire to your bed space and hut, where your bed pack and utensils were inspected for cleanliness. If the CO discovered any dust or dirt then the POW was put on 'fatigues' and given extra duties. I don't think there was ever a clear round; there were always a few who fell foul and ended up doing the extra chores that were needed done in the compound. Paul Hoey claimed he held the record for the most fatigues during his imprisonment, but none of us believed him.

We were getting quite good at drilling and Danny would put us through our paces every afternoon, teaching us new drill movements, which we began to like and looked forward too. Every prisoner was given the task of getting a uniform and marching boots into the camp. Our organisations on the outside got us all surplus British Army boots, which we had sent in over a period of weeks so as not to arouse any suspicion. We were also expected to get dark trousers, a black polo neck or shirt and black jacket. However the prison authorities caught on to this and banned black shirts and black polo necks from the camp. Not to be deterred, we just got white shirts in and dyed them black, and any colour of polo neck sweater and dyed them black also. Visitors would wear black jackets and then swap them with prisoners on visits. In a few months we all had a uniform.

Our boots became our pride and joy; we had to sit and bull them just like soldiers of WWI and II. Bull was sometimes known as 'spit and polish' and involved rubbing a damp cloth, water and polish in a small, circular fashion into marching boots, especially around the toecaps and heels. Groups of us young, raw recruits would sit and polish our boots for hours until we could see our reflections. There were a few old soldiers in the compound who would show us how to bring them up to an immaculate standard, such as Big John, a member of the 'Chindits', who fought in the jungles of Burma against the Japanese. We would sit round his bed space and he would tell us old yarns about his war days as we polished our boots. To cap it all off we smuggled in spar balls to insert in the sole of our boots to make that sharp clicking noise as we marched.

The next stage was to smuggle in cloth materials to make flags for a colour party. The materials were systematically smuggled in and we created union flags, regimental flags, UVF and RHC flags, using the sewing machine we had for handicrafts. Belts and flag holders were made from leather crafts and we made cap comforters with the knitting machine we also had for handicrafts.

The Nissen huts in each compound were numbered by the prison but we replaced them with plagues renaming them Somme, Passchendaele and Ypres after the battles of WWI.

Finally, when we went on parade. Soldiers, prison officers and Republicans would come to watch us parade in our uniforms and colour party. When I reflect on this period, it is clear that it brought us all together and created discipline and cleanliness of the highest standard. It created comradeship and pride, and helped us all get through such a difficult period in our lives. It also earned respect from other factions and the prison authorities.

CHAPTER 8

The Ghost Television

OVER THE CHRISTMAS period prisoners worked out a rota so that Christmas visits, which were limited, would be prioritised for prisoners who were married and had children. We were building up stores of food purchased from the prison shop. Handicraft material for making leather wallets and all the accessories had to be brought on visits after getting permission from the prison governor. Trying to build up some kind of library was a priority. We had one letter per week and one A4 sheet to write on. The letters were heavily censored so prisoners could not really express their true thoughts or personal feeling in their letters. Any private information or communications were smuggled out through visits. So we were anxious to get the Christmas period over and get on with fighting for a humane and productive prison regime.

UDA prisoners were in one hut under the leadership of Jimmy Craig, UVF/RHC in another and the third hut was shared. The fourth hut was used as a canteen. The canteen hut was filled with a hot plate, table and chairs and at the back of the hut was a television. When we were locked up at night the canteen was locked up and the TV remained in the canteen. Gusty negotiated that the TV should be allowed to be taken out of the canteen at night and shared between the huts over Christmas Eve, Christmas Day and Boxing Day. This proved very popular so we negotiated for a further three days over the New Year period and this was granted also. We requested that a TV be installed in each hut but the Governor refused this request. We even offered to buy our own TVs but this was also refused. However, never underestimate the ingenuity of prisoners in captivity.

Prisoners noticed that when the prison officers were locking up the canteen they didn't check the TV, they just looked up the hut to see it was there. One prisoner came up with the idea of making a replica TV. Some of the beds we had been issued had Formica foot and headboards, out of which he meticulously constructed a replica TV. Fifteen minutes before the prison officers came into the compound to lock us up, a number of prisoners would replace the real TV with the replica. A rota system was set up so that each hut got a turn and the real TV was sneaked into the designated hut. We would huddle round the TV, keeping the sound down and blacking out the windows with spare blankets. Everyone enjoyed the set up and it was much better knowing we were getting one over the authorities. Before we were unlocked in the morning we would switch them around again.

We got away with this for months, dismantling the replica when searches were due so that it would not be detected. Of course nothing lasts forever. A world title fight was due on TV at the weekend and it would not be shown until the early hours of the morning. Jimmy Craig, UDA Commander was an ex-boxer and pleaded with Gusty to allow his hut to have the TV that night even though it was not his turn. Gusty agreed to his request. So Jimmy was well pleased and he was looking forward to the fight. Later that night he was watching the boxing match and in his excitement he turned the TV volume up too loud. In the early hours of the morning the sound travelled further than usual and two prison officers walking round the outside of the compound were suspicious of the sounds. They entered the compound, opened the canteen hut and were baffled at first when they saw a TV sitting on the top table. They walked up to TV and plugged it in, and it was only when they turned the knobs to turn it on, which came off in their hands, that they realised something was wrong. They then opened the back of the TV and found there was nothing there and immediately phoned their superiors. Unfortunately for us, the Camp Kommandant was on duty. Within half an hour we were awoken with the noise of marching boots and the barking of war dogs. The Governor was in his glory shouting at us to come out and line up against the wire perimeter of the compound. As we emerged from our huts, hundreds of soldiers in full riot gear and war dogs pushed us along, shouting at us to get against the wire. I thought for sure we were going to get a beating, but then I suppose even the Governor couldn't justify a riot over a TV. They searched the huts, wrecking our beds and throwing our personal belongings all over the place. They emerged with a TV and the Governor ranted and raved about how he was in control and how he would smash any kind of insubordination. They locked us up and marched away into the night.

CHAPTER 9

Internment

WE HAD JUST been locked up in our huts on 2 February 1973, when about half an hour later we could hear the locks of the doors being opened again and we thought we were going to get a surprise search. We did get a surprise. Two people walked into the hut. They were Leonard McCreery and Bertie Halsall, the first two Loyalists to be interned in Northern Ireland. Now this posed another problem for the authorities, as they were internees amongst sentenced prisoners. Long Kesh was now the main prison for sentenced prisoners, remand prisoners and now Loyalist internees as well as Republican internees. We made them feel welcome and gave them food, cigarettes and anything else they needed. We had a long chat with them because we didn't fully understand this new concept of 'Internment of Loyalists'. What we did understand was that the huts in Compound 12 were bursting at the seams with the growing population.

The prison authorities, in their usual Victorian splendour, were greatly upset by the fact that internees were in the same hut as sentenced prisoners. They had to be treated differently. Such was their concern that they provided them with different meals, steel knives and forks, and Delph plates. At meal times the food truck would appear at the compound gates and there would be meals for all us sentenced prisoners and two separate meals of better quality for the two internees. Sentenced prisoners were locked up at 9.00 pm but internees were locked up at 10.00 pm, so Bertie and Leonard had an extra hour walking round the compound. The whole situation was becoming ridiculous. In the following weeks more Loyalists were interned and the prison quickly moved Official IRA prisoners out of Compound 11 and moved in the Loyalist internees. So for a while the Prison authorities felt redeemed. They seemed to have a moral dilemma having sentenced prisoners and internees in the same compound. .

A press photograph, which includes me, showing "A unit of the Special Services Command, Red Hand Action Group on foot patrol in Beresford Street, off the Shankill Road".

This is my very first photograph in Long Kesh, in August 1972, when I applied for a driving licence. I had convinced the Governor that the prison should be responsible for taking the picture.

Myself with Ronnie McCullough in Long Kesh in 1972.

In the early days of the muster parades most of us wore our casual clothes and footwear.

Despite the casual attire we still drilled and marched.

One of the earliest activities was weapons training with replica weapons we made within the prison. Here prisoners pose with a replica machine gun.

Left to right: Jim Irvine (Commander Compound 19), Tommy Cull and Danny Strutt. Cull and Strutt both escaped from Crumlin Road Prison and upon their recapture were moved to Long Kesh.

Within months of arriving in Long Kesh we had either smuggled in or made our own uniforms consisting of dark trousers, a black polo neck or shirt and a black jacket.

A group of prisoners pose in their homemade uniforms.

Personal cleanliness and cleanliness of the huts was of a very high standard, with bed spaces, plates and cutlery washed and set out on the beds beside bed packs ready for inspection.

All emblems and flags were made inside the prison with materials smuggled during visits.

Marching was practiced daily to a very high standard and on muster parades it was full uniform and inspection.

Gusty Spence was determined that most of us would leave the camp as better men and sought to stimulate our minds with lectures as an alternative to weapons training.

Gusty held political and historical classes in the compounds to encourage prisoners to gainfully spend their days in confinement.

Classes in English language were also in great demand as most of the prisoners' outside contact was through letter writing.

During protests with the prison authorities we set up a quarter guard that patrolled the inside of the compounds to prevent a surprise attack by riot squads.

Prisoners relaxing with a game of cards.

With only one smuggled-in camera per compound, group photographs became popular.

Another group of prisoners posing for a picture in a blind spot in the compound.

A group photograph featuring the late David Ervine (rear row, first from left), future leader of the Progressive Unionist Party (PUP) and MLA, and Gusty Spence (rear row, third from left), Officer Commanding within Long Kesh.

Christmas dinner in the compounds.

When Loyalist sentenced prisoners and internees were separated into different compounds we were only able to speak to them when we went down to play in the football pitches which were beside their compound.

Jim Craig commander of UDA prisoners along with other UDA prisoners.

Football was very popular amongst most prisoners,
including myself, seen kneeling in the bottom photograph.

A group of 'Liverpool' supporters proudly pose.

Another image of prisoners, including David Ervine standing fifth from left.

HM ~~Prison Maze~~ Lisburn Co Antrim

PRISONER OF WAR Camp.
MAZE.

14 December 1972

WEEKLY PARCEL FOR "~~A~~ ~~WING~~ PRISONERS

S/CATEGORY

200 Cigarettes or 6 ozs Tobacco
1 lb Sweets or 4 Bars Chocolate
4 lbs Fruit
Tissues (small packets sealed)
1 Bar Toilet Soap
1 Tube Toothpaste
1 Toothbrush
3 Shampoos (sachets only)
1 Stick Shaving Soap or 1 Tube Shaving Cream
1 Comb (plastic)

1 lb Butter
½ lb Cheese
1 lb Biscuits (loose)
1 Cake (quartered before issue)
1 Bottle Sauce
1 lb Cooked Meats (sliced)
1 Chicken (quartered)

BREADS

4 Farls (soda or wheaten)
2 packets Potato Bread

NB Every parcel must contain a list of its contents

Should a prisoner not receive parcels from outside, the equivalent amount (as above) can be purchased from the canteen.

Anything other than the above articles will be confiscated.

A. Colton s/o

Political prisoners were allowed a weekly parcel into the prison once per week. It was a meagre list however it supplemented the prison food. The list displayed on prison notice boards illustrates the daily battle of minds as prisoners scribble out "HMP Maze" and wrote "Prisoner of War Camp".

The political pressure had been growing since 1972 when Internment was introduced, as thus far only Nationalists had been interned. The sectarian card was being played by Nationalists and now, to appear to be even handed, the British were balancing the books by having Loyalists interned. The arrests were based solely on the British government being seen to be impartial. Protestants were being interned, including a teacher, a manager of construction firm and a general catchment of Protestants with the flimsiest of excuses. Morally, we disagreed with Internment from the start, and we also knew that sooner or later the British would, under pressure, turn towards Protestants. Recently released government papers prove that was the case.

Seventeen Protestants have lodged claims for compensation against the British Government due them from being interned in the 70s. During a trawl by their legal counsel of government documents held in the National Archives at Kew Gardens, there were references of the need to intern Protestants. By late 1972, memos began to circulate in the Ministry of Defence and Northern Ireland Office as to when and under which circumstances they might arrest and intern Protestants. One document was sub-titled 'Arrest Policy for Protestants' and marked secret. It stated:

> This policy does not provide for the arrest of Protestant terrorists except with the object of bringing a criminal charge. Protestants are not, as the policy stands, arrested with the view to their being the subject to Interim Custody Orders. Ministers have judged that the time at the moment is not ripe for an extension of the arrest policy in respect of Protestants.

In a letter from Secretary of State William Whitelaw to Lt Gen Sir Harry Tuzo HQ Northern Ireland, dated 6 November 1972, he outlines the criteria for Internment orders and that Loyalists "may fall" within the new order.

On 8 December 1972, in a memo written by AW Stephens, MOD London and circulated among various departments, he refers to a meeting at Stormont on 29 November 1972 where the GOC was asked to draft an arrest policy covering UVF and other extreme Loyalist elements.

On the 7 February, four days after the first Loyalists were interned, WKK White from the Foreign and Commonwealth Office, London wrote to KC Thom Esquire, Dublin:

we assume that you are content with the service you are getting from Northern Ireland on such matters of the arrests and now the Internment – the latter very helpful politically – of Protestants.

Internees were put in an intolerable position legally. They didn't know how long they would be detained, they didn't know what the charges were against them and they didn't know what evidence, if any, was being offered by the authorities. However, they got on with things as best as they could and mixed in with the sentenced prisoners as much as possible. They participated in education classes, handicrafts and other pastimes. Republicans had been interned from the 9 August 1971, and had undergone a substantial period of time in Long Kesh. The world-wide outcry against 'Interment without Trial' grew rapidly from the moment it was introduced, and the British, being British, thought that by introducing the facade of a Commissioners' Courts, in November 1972, they could lessen the criticism by calling it 'Detention with Trial'.

The Commissioners' Courts where held in huts in the camp and were presided over by a retired English Judge. The internee would receive an Interim Custody Order that covered his interment. After a period in custody he would receive a paper containing allegations, but not actual charges. At the makeshift camp courts there would be the commissioner, the prosecutor, the internee, his solicitor and barrister. A large screen was erected from behind where a 'witness' (usually a police inspector) would give evidence.

For example, William D was arrested at 5.45 am on Friday 9 March 1973 from his home on the Shankill Road. He was married with baby twin daughters. He had never been arrested nor had any type of brush with the law before then. He was taken to Ladas Drive Interrogation Centre and was served with an Interim Custody Order. This order was issued by the Secretary of State under the Detention of Terrorists (Northern Ireland) Order 1972.

The Secretary of State in pursuance of Article 4(1) hereby orders the detention of William D.

Being a person suspected of having been concerned in the commission or attempted commission of an act of terrorism or in the direction, organisation or training of persons for the purpose of terrorism.

The person aforesaid shall not be detained under this Order for more than 28 days unless the case is referred to a Commissioner for determination.

Dated this day 11th March 1973

Signed William Whitelaw
ONE OF HER MAJESTY'S PRINCIPAL
SECRETARIES OF STATE
To the Governor or other person in charge of HM Prison, The Maze
To the said William D.

William D had been working in a major plumbing, heating and electrical engineers firm for 27 years prior to his arrest. He was employed as job designer, doing job costing, labour hire and finalising accounts. When arrested he was in complete charge of a contract then valued at £400,000.

He was a member of a pipe band, a chairman and drum instructor for 22 years. He sat on the Advisory Committee of the Scottish Pipe Band Association both in Belfast and Glasgow. He was a drumming judge in North Belfast and at St Finbars in Cork, travelling to Cork once a month, where he was hosted by a member of the band. When he received his allegations on 23 April 1973, that he had caused an explosion and robbed book-makers, he was somewhat bewildered. They read:

1) That you being a member of the UVF, were concerned with the commission of the following acts of terrorism in Belfast, namely:
   a) With others on the 12th February, 1973, caused an explosion at the Kingsway Bar, Smithfield.
   b) With others on 17th February, 1973, were concerned in an armed robbery at the premises of Smyths Betting Office, Agnes Street.

He appeared in front of the Commissioners' Court on 8 June 1973 where the Commissioner ruled that his continued detention was necessary for the protection of the public. At the beginning of the tribunal, William D made his objections to this 'kangaroo court' abundantly clear.

Your Honour,
I would like the following statement to be recorded as I am not satisfied with the method used by the Crown in order to have me interned.
I WD have today seen British justice practiced in its most obnoxious form in this courtroom whereby an honest and innocent person without a blemish on his character has been sentenced to a period of Internment

on the word of a paid informer who by his very nature must be a man of low moral standards.

And you, your honour, with all due respect, by participating in this legal charade must surely bring the whole of the British judicial system into disrepute in the eyes of the world and must cause abhorrence to ordinary people and those engaged in the legal profession who still believe that British justice stands for a man being innocent until proven guilty in a court of law.

Your honour, I would like to end this statement by asking all the people concerned in this farce, are they the convicted by having to resort to the use of manufactured evidence in order to convict, or am I the innocent by being subjected to such a mockery of a trial.

Gentlemen only you can give the correct answer to this statement.

William D also requested transcripts of trial in relation to appeal and if no transcripts provided, then recourse to facilities for manufacturing own transcripts.

He was finally released on the 18 June 1974, 15 months after his arrest. He told me that although he was able to return to his job, he was never promoted and lost out on a lot of prospects before he eventually left the company.

Ken Gibson was another such unfortunate, arrested in June 1973 and brought before the Commissioners' Court. He was alleged to be a senior member of the UVF on the word of an anonymous paid informer. An 'Officer A' in the RUC confirmed that he knew the informer and was certain he was of a sound character. The barrister was told he couldn't ask any questions regarding the informer as this could put him in danger. The Commissioner stated that the Officer could reveal the evidence to him but he would invoke Paragraph 17 of the Act, which meant that the internee and his legal team would have to leave the court and he would hear the evidence in their absence. Despite many attempts by the learned barrister Desmond Boal, the charade proved impossible to circumvent. Ken became a Detainee. Now we had three different types of prisoners between Compounds 11 and 12: special category, internees and detainees. The official total number of Protestants/Loyalists arrested and interned was 107.

CHAPTER 10

Conveyor Belt to Prison

THE VIOLENCE ON the outside continued and the stream of new prisoners kept filling up the prisons. It wasn't long before Compound 12 was spilling over, so we negotiated to move some of the overflow from 12 into 11. Gusty asked for ten Volunteers to move, and myself and Ronnie McCullough went with Gusty to Compound 11 to help set up a new structure within. One hut housed internees, one was UDA and the other UVF/RHC. However, the authorities still treated the internees different. Two food trucks arrived at meal times, one for the internees and one for the sentenced prisoners. We were locked up at 9.00 pm they were locked up at 10.00 pm. However, there were advantages being in the same compound with internees. They could get a visit every day so communication with the outside was improved tenfold. They could get a food parcel every day so they would let us get extra food parcels in their name. They were allowed as much money in their accounts as they wanted so we could get more money in their name. This allowed us to buy more food stuffs from the prison shop. They also could get as much writing paper and write as many letters as they wanted. We could only get one A4 sheet and one letter per week, so we could now get extra paper from them. In a matter of a few months we went from one compound to two compounds and there was no sign of the population boom ending.

On the 15 August 1972 Jim Irvine, James Strutt, Thomas Cull and Norman Sayers appeared in front of Belfast Courts charged with armed robbery. They became the first Loyalists to refuse to recognise a British Court in protest at the proroguing of the Northern Ireland Parliament at Stormont and the imposition of Direct Rule from Westminster. Jim Irvine addressed the courts on behalf of the four stating, "As volunteers in the Ulster Volunteer Force we refuse to recognise this court as it is an instrument of an illegal and undemocratic regime". Trevor King was another member of the UVF to refuse to recognise the Courts in protest to Direct Rule. Their address shows how Loyalists deliberately worded their statements to be different from those of IRA prisoners, by emphasising their reasons as a result of Direct Rule being imposed in Northern Ireland. This policy continued for a few months but was discontinued due to lack of support and influence.

In August 1973 the 'Diplock Courts', named after Lord Diplock, were introduced. These courts removed the right of trial by a jury, changed the rules of evidence and abolished the judge's rules. One judge would preside over a trial, acting as judge and jury. This was seen as a further dilution of justice and a preparatory step by the British for when Internment would inevitably end. The introduction of these courts, which degraded the quality of evidence and shifted the onus of proof onto the accused, rapidly increased the prison population further. This also posed a dilemma for Loyalists as to what policy they would adopt, as Republicans chose to refuse to recognise the court. This was a predicament that Loyalists found themselves in on many occasions, where they agreed with the principle of human rights and justice but found themselves unable to jointly oppose violations of those rights along with Republicans, else they would be labelled as siding with the enemy. Loyalists therefore had an open policy that if the accused believed he could fight the charges he could do so – otherwise he would refuse to recognise the court (see Appendix 2). The first Loyalist to refuse to recognise the Diplock Court was an East Belfast UDA member, William Sloan, who read a book about the 'B' Specials the whole way through the trial. He later became the commander of UDA prisoners in the camp. Eventually this policy was abandoned and everyone was given the freedom to make up their own mind. Later on, Republicans also abandoned their policy. The first prisoner to plead 'Not Guilty' in a Diplock Court and be found 'Guilty' was Loyalist Winston Rea.

CHAPTER 11

No Entry

THE PRISON POPULATION was now bursting at the seams and the administration of the compounds became a headache for prison authorities, prisoners and the organisations on the outside. There were basically no clear cut rules as to who was eligible to come into the compounds and who was not. To the prison authorities, they simply acted upon the request of a sentenced prisoner and sent them to Long Kesh irrespective of the offence they had committed. As long as a prisoner had been convicted under the Scheduled Offences Act to a term of nine months or more they were acceptable for entry into the compounds. We disagreed of course and insisted that the leadership inside the compounds would decide who was acceptable into the compound structure. The command structure on the inside and outside came up with a set of rules and regulations that would have to be met before a prisoner would be allowed into the Loyalists' compounds of Long Kesh:

1) Prisoners would have to be claimed by their relevant organisation or in the case of members of the Orange Volunteer Force, Tara or Ulster Protestant Volunteers through adoption by either the UVF/RHC or UDA.
2) Prisoners claiming Special Category Status would need to prove their operation was sanctioned by the relevant organisation. (This of course was not watertight as it depended on the honesty and integrity of the commanders on the outside.)
3) Prisoners who made statements to the security forces revealing names or compromising the security of the organisation were classed as informers and banned from compounds.
4) Prisoners would have to undergo a court of inquiry where they would be questioned by senior officers in the camp and produce their court deposition papers. This action protected the security of the organisations both inside and outside the prison.

Even though we made the camp authorities aware of these rules they refused to recognise our entry criteria and the issue came to a head in May 1973.

The previous July (1972), as bonfires where being lit all over Northern Ireland, four men entered a house in Southport Street in the Oldpark Road area of Belfast. The house was occupied by a Catholic widow Mrs McClenaghan and her 14-year-old disabled son David McClenaghan. Also in the house was a male Protestant lodger. One of the four men had a gun and threatened everyone in the house. They interrogated and battered the occupants, accusing them of being spies, and of having weapons and being supporters of the IRA.

Mrs McClenaghan later gave evidence that she was awakened by the sound of glass breaking and a shot being fired. When she went downstairs she was confronted by these four men, three of whom had their faces masked while the fourth man with the gun was barefaced. They forced her son David to get his mother's handbag, which he did, and when he brought it back they found a set of rosary beads and removed any money from the bag. They then ordered the boy to go upstairs while two of the men subjected his mother to a brutal sexual assault. After they had committed their assault they took the mother back upstairs and forced her onto the bed beside her son David. She started screaming and pleading with the men but the man with the gun pointed it at her son David and shot him three times, and as she threw her body over her son to protect him the gunman also shot her three times. David died but his mother survived. The Protestant lodger was beaten and tortured with a cigarette lighter but survived.

In the depravity and brutality of Belfast in 1972, as word swept the area of the sadistic murder and rape, the whole of the Protestant community was enraged at the actions of their co-religionists. In the tightly knit Protestant community, it wasn't long before the assailants had been identified and became known to local paramilitaries. An active service unit was dispatched, with orders to assassinate the gunman immediately. The active service unit burst into home of the gunman prepared to dispense their own justice, but their quarry had escaped. The next day the other three men handed themselves in to the local police station and were immediately charged. In May 1973 they were tried before a jury and convicted of their abhorrent crimes. The gunman, who was arrested a few days later, requested to be put under protection as he had already been sentenced to death by the organisations on the outside and spent all his time awaiting trial under protective custody. The other three men however, were to be sent to the compounds. The leadership in the camp were united in their opposition to the men being allowed into the compounds to serve their sentences and notified the prison authorities of their opposition. The prison authorities ignored this and insisted that they would put them where they thought they should be. The prison authorities were then informed that the safety of the men could not be guaranteed but they chose to ignore this also. Their attitude was all to do with who controlled the camp and who didn't.

A week after three of the men were sentenced they were moved from Crumlin Road Prison to Long Kesh Camp. After lock up we heard the gates being opened in Compound 11 and then the doors of two of the huts. One man was put into one large hut and the other two into the half-hut, which was split between accommodation and handicrafts. They were not touched during the hours of lock up as we would all have been complicit. The next morning the prison officers opened the doors and we went about our normal routines without showing any signs of outward antagonism. As was customary, newly committed prisoners would appear before the Governor and be read the rules regulations and riot act. The three prisoners were due to meet the governor at 10.30 am. At 10.00 am three units of four men each entered into the huts concerned and began systematically beating the men ruthlessly with iron bed ends and bars. There was no mercy shown and one of the men had his legs smashed with a fire extinguisher. The senior officers then called a halt to the beatings and at 10.15 am the three men, screaming and groaning in agony, were placed on blankets, dragged out of the huts along the compound tarmac and left at the gates of the compound in time for their appointment with the Governor. When they were being dragged to the gates of Compound 11, Republican prisoners in surrounding compounds stood along the wire and clapped at the actions of the Loyalists. I don't gloat over this situation. It was brutal and ruthless but that's the way it was. The prisoner authorities didn't respond to the cries and moans of the injured prisoners as they lay at the gates, and it took an hour to get them to hospital and be treated. Needless to say, after that the prison authorities recognised who had the veto over who came into the prison and who didn't.

CHAPTER 12

The Political Think Tank

THE OPEN DEBATES about history and politics manifested themselves in the formation of a political think tank. It was made up of prisoners who showed more than a casual interest in debating the political future of Northern Ireland and in how to formulate some type of political settlement that would lead to an end to the war. At first there were about ten of us who gathered twice weekly in the study hut and put forward ideas and suggestions to be discussed. The think tank was comprised of Gusty, myself, R McCullough and a compliment of internees, Ken Gibson, William Davidson, George Orr and John McKeague. This mixture of UVF/RHC prisoners and internees debated the hard issues amongst themselves and sought out opinions from other prisoners. In March 1973 we had a seminar in which everybody who wanted to sat in and threw out various options that we felt could be discussed, however absurd or offensive it might be.

A Statement of Intent

As we read the situation the Loyalists of Ulster have four alternatives;

1) The Assembly of Northern Ireland working
2) Dominion Status
3) An All Ireland
4) Unilateral Declaration of Independence

We state unequivocally and categorically that the number three alternative, (All Ireland Republic) if forced upon us would certainly lead to civil war and we would forthwith use every and any means necessary to oppose this imposition. The outcome would be too dreadful to contemplate. We are also of the opinion that an all Ireland Republic is not practically feasible simply because the Free State Government would not relish the thought of one third of the population bearing arms against the state and the British Government being fearful that war would undoubtedly spreading to the mainland.[1]

We are however inclined to think that the number one option (the Northern Ireland Assembly working as a unit) could be the short term answer to our problems. Much would depend on the good will and foresight of those participating in the assembly, and taking this as our premise we put forward the following proposals, which we contend will be conducive to the Northern Ireland Assembly getting off the ground.

1) We suggest that the term 'power sharing' is a contentious and emotive phrase and we prefer to use and have accepted the phrase 'Equal Responsibility', the reason being that one cannot have authority without responsibility and vice versa. We do agree that there must be devolution of power and the minority must have access to dual responsibility and authority. We contend that, when every avenue of grievance is removed from the complaint board, they probably shall have no other alternative but to co-operate and for those reasons, present radical proposals may not seem at all radical when viewed in that context.

2) In the event of an all Ireland Council being constituted we would oppose any presumption for that council to legislate for the people of Northern Ireland in any context except Tourism, Electricity, Regional Development and some Agricultural aspect of Development. We would view the all Ireland Council as being similar to the boundary commission constituted in 1925.

3) The particular grievance uppermost in the minority complaints appears to be the RUC. We would not be opposed to a limited form of reconstruction of this service. However, the reconstruction would not have to be seen as an instrument of appeasement to the minority and so serve as to explode the confidence of the men serving in the service. Beyond a doubt the job of the police is to detect the

---

1 At first this may seem negative but here we are in 1973, in the cold barren wastes of an Internment camp amongst 'Loyalist Terrorists' and they are:
a) Putting an all Ireland option on the agenda.
b) Discussing that option and giving it air time.
c) Showing to be non-discriminatory in that they were prepared to bear arms against the British and the Irish Governments.

criminal, apprehend him and place him before the courts, as opposed to employment of a political nature. The Special Branch should be geared to those duties the same as their counterparts in Great Britain. We have no argument against the police and UDR under the direct control of the Westminster Government.

4) We deem it necessary that the Roman Catholic Church will pronounce to the effect that it will sever or at least deny any political links that they may have with any political party.

5) Commencing with the various teaching colleges encompassing both ends of the political and religious spectrum, we would suggest that the Assembly or Government should enact a Bill that would permit a merger within two years of a general ceasefire coming into force in Northern Ireland. It is logical to assume that any form of Integration that may or will come about would be first made operable amongst the adults within the teaching vocation. In the long term the contended view is that after five years of a ceasefire coming into operation, a further Bill be drafted and enacted making it possible for secular schools to replace the systems of schooling we now have in Northern Ireland, with full facilities for religious instruction. In short a fully integrated school system to wipe away the memories of past bitterness and injustice. When the Bill would be enacted and about a further five years later we would envisage full compensation to those authorities responsible to the original school building. The private system of schooling would not be objectionable provided that it was along the same lines to that now operational in England and not at public expense. There is obvious room for manoeuvre by anyone who would wish to revert to the old segregated system but this would obviously be resisted in the drafting of the two proposed Bills.[2]

6) There is less of a problem when one looks at our hospital system and we think that with good sense and inspired negotiation there is no reason why a Universal Hospital system cannot evolve. It would be imperative that the free flow of qualified persons of whatever denomination be encouraged between hospitals and medical colleges.[3]

---

2 Even then, we as prisoners of the conflict knew that the key to the future lay with our children and the biggest hurdle to that was segregated education. Even our teaching colleges were segregated along religious lines so we thought the adults should lead by example.

3 Although the hospitals treated everyone there was that divide between the management of National Health hospitals and the Catholic sponsored hospitals. That did eventually change due to funding pressure rather than the need.

Removed from the day to day chaos of conflict on the outside we were able to discuss, debate and produce a document tackling core issues in a mature and open handed manner without the fear of being called a traitor or coward. These proposals for integrated education, realisation of moving forward and mending the failures of the past shows great foresight and courage by the prisoners to even put these topics on the agenda for discussion.

The camp at that time held some of the most senior members of the UVF/RHC and the 'Camp Council' and 'political think tank' had significant influence on political and operational matters on the outside. The co-operation between factions demonstrated by the Camp Council led to discussions about the possibility of talks between armed groups on the outside. The 'political think tank' drafted suggested possible points of discussion geared towards bringing about a universal and permanent ceasefire. These proposals were sent out to brigade staff of the UVF/RHC to be ratified. The brigade staff discussed the proposals at length and they were finally endorsed by a vote of 4–2 majority. Billy Mitchell and another member of brigade staff travelled to County Westmeath for exploratory talks with David O'Connell and Brian Keenan. They were held in a fishing lodge on Lough Sheelin and armed members of PIRA provided security. The talks skirted around a few subjects but Billy Mitchell informed the PIRA delegation that the UVF/RHC had accepted basically the principle of 'equal responsibility' in government and were prepared to discuss it. Other issues raised were the ongoing sectarian violence, the term used by PIRA of 'economic targets' which proverbially meant Protestant businesses and the targeting of off duty UDR men. The PIRA delegation was comfortable with the term 'equal responsibility' and agreed to explore the issue of targets. The delegations agreed to report back to their relevant groups and meet the following Monday in Dundalk to discuss a meeting with wider delegations, possibly five from each side. A few weeks later a meeting was held in County Cavan. Billy Mitchell again led the UVF/RHC delegation with four other members of brigade staff in attendance. The PIRA delegation consisted of David O'Connell, Brian Keenan, Seamus Twomey, O'Neill and Martin McGuinness. An armed unit of PIRA again provided security. The main issues raised by the UVF/RHC delegation were:

a) The targeting of shops, bakeries, small businesses and properties as part of the PIRA economic bombing campaign.

b) A safety committee made up of Sandy Scott, Rector John Stewart, Father

Murphy and a representative of the Quaker organisation to be constituted and work with armed groups to prevent sectarian assassinations.

c) Political settlement.

d) The targeting of off-duty UDR men.

On points A, B, and D there was support for these points with a caveat that both delegations return to their relative organisations and that while there was no agreement on point C, there was agreement to dither.

There was also a meeting with the Official IRA. Billy Mitchell and Jim Hanna met with Billy McMillen and Desi O'Hagan for exploratory talks in the Old House, Albert Street in West Belfast. Arrangements were then made to meet in Dublin with Billy Mitchell leading the UVF/RHC delegation of four people while the OIRA were represented by Cathal Goulding, Garland and Desi O'Hagan. This meeting was more comfortable than that with PIRA. The issues were pretty broad and acceptable to both delegations:

a) An end to sectarian killings in the North.

b) Working class unity.

c) Anti-internment moves.

d) Acceptance of Northern Ireland as part of the United Kingdom for the foreseeable future.

All these subjects were discussed maturely with very little disagreement and further meetings were contemplated to discuss the issues again.

When we got a report and record of the meetings we were delighted that they had gone so well and we were hopeful that there could be a breakthrough in the war. Unfortunately our hopes were short lived. These groundbreaking and courageous steps to bring the conflict to an end were scuppered when the media got word of the meetings being held. The window of opportunity to bring an end to the conflict was closed and our people, our country would have to wait two more decades and over 2,000 more lost lives before that window would open again.

Gradually we were able to compose a political document in 1974 which we called 'Sharing Responsibility', note not power, but responsibility. Many of us found the document progressive, the goals possible, and all of it based on the principals of equality and human rights. We called a meeting of all the prisoners together and had a full and frank debate on the merits or demerits of the draft document. Prisoners were free to express whatever opinions they had on the politics of the country and the suggestions we had put together. There was a wide and varied debate on the issues and while some agreed on the document's sentiments, some were diametrically opposed and others were selective. No matter what their views were, they all got the opportunity to express them without fear or favour. We of the 'political think tank' were actually impressed by the response of the prisoners. It was mature and straightforward, and it also gave us a lot to think about, so it was back to the drawing board, determined and not disheartened. We amended sections, introduced new ones, tweaked and tweaked at it until we believed we had a formidable and challenging way forward. Here are some of the proposals:

a) To secure peace and reconciliation within this region of the United Kingdom.
b) To establish a local administration in this region, representative of all interested parties and groups.
c) To actively work for political, social and economic advancements to secure a better life for all our people.
d) To pursue new and established policies through a broadly representative committee system of government.
e) The financial arrangements for the regional administration should be such as to give Northern Ireland both its fair share of United Kingdom resources and a certain flexibility with regard to revenue and expenditure.
f) A Bill of Rights of Northern Ireland should embody a Bill of Rights along the lines of the European Convention on Human Rights which would include guarantees against discrimination.
g) Economic co-operation with a European Member State, cross border or North/South co-operation.

In 1974 the document was finalised and sent to the brigade staff to be ratified. The document was then updated in 1977, 1979, 1980, 1984 and 1985. In 1998, 24 years after it was first penned in Long Kesh, it became the basis for the Progressive Unionist Party at the negotiations that led to the Good Friday Agreement.

The political soundings in the compounds were reaching the ears of Government and in April 1974 Merlyn Rees, Secretary of State, announced that he would de-proscribe the UVF/RHC and Sinn Féin and also phase out Internment. A month later, the UVF/RHC and Sinn Féin were legalised and

Rees announced the gradual phasing out of internment officially in the House of Commons.

In June 1975 David Ervine entered into the compounds of Long Kesh. I didn't know Davy until he came in but he took to life in the compounds like a duck to water. He participated in everything – drill, physical training, education and handicrafts. He was very popular and he had a personality which harmonised with every other prisoner. When he heard about our 'Political Think Tank' he was right in there participating with enthusiasm and delight. I think the freedom of thought and expression allowed in the compounds warmed his heart and he and I had some intense and imaginative arguments. However, Davy never held any grudges against anyone and just came back to the next meeting as enthusiastic as ever.

CHAPTER 13

The Swap

SINCE WE HAD split up into separate huts upon arrival from Crumlin Road, relationships between the UVF/RHC and the UDA had gradually deteriorated. People who I was born and bred with had retreated behind this invisible wall of factions. Now as I walked round the compound I could barely get a hello from them. There were now three Loyalist compounds: C11, C12 and C19. Both Gusty and UDA leader Jimmy Craig had made numerous requests to the Governor to have separate compounds but it fell on deaf ears. Jimmy and Gusty had been able to settle any disputes that had arisen thus far, but they knew that might not always be possible in the future.

Relationships between the organisations on the outside had also deteriorated and obviously this found its way into the camp. Jimmy and Gusty were both in C19, part of Phase 6, while C11 and C12 were some distance away in Phase 5. If any disputes happened in C11 or C12 Gusty and Jimmy might have gotten there too late to nip it in the bud and God knows how serious it could have become. They both came to the same conclusion that due to the reluctance of the authorities to accede to our request, we would have to take some form of action by ourselves. They toiled over the situation in their minds because the options in confinement are limited and once you decide to fight then you're fighting the British Army and you have nowhere to run. Gusty and Jimmy finally came up with what they thought was best action in the circumstances. If the authorities wouldn't separate us then we would separate ourselves. It was either fight each other or the British Army. The British Army drew the short straw.

All commanding officers of each organisation had negotiated freedom of travel between compounds through the Camp Council. The authorities saw this extension of movement between compounds as a useful tool to settle arguments or disputes but it also could be used for other things. Gusty and

Jimmy as COs requested to visit C11 and C12 to reveal their cunning plan. On arrival at C11 they met the joint leadership of both the UDA and UVF/RHC and told them of the situation and their concerns about possible feuds breaking out between the organisations on the inside and maybe leading to fatalities. The authorities had pushed them into a corner and they suggested that joint action needed to be taken. The proposal was that the compound gates were to be commandeered and UDA men in C11 would swap to C12, while simultaneously UVF/RHC men in C12 would swap to C11. C19 would be put on standby too and were to be ready to go over the wire should any brutality or mistreatment occur. We were in Phase 6 so technically the only prisoners we could swap with were the Officials of the Provos and that didn't sound plausible. Semaphorists would remain on the hut roofs during any ensuing riot. They then went to C12 and delivered the same message. The officers in both compounds were left to work out the nuts and bolts of how they would commandeer the compound and how they would carry out the swap. Meetings of all the men were then discreetly called and they were informed of the proposed action. Everyone to a man backed the proposals without question. Everyone understood that we had no other choice in the present circumstances.

There were prisoners inside who could spot cracks in stainless steel and it wasn't too long before the plans were laid before the officers. The one sure thing about the British penal system or the British military is that they work with predictable precision. They do the same thing at the same time in the same way every day. It was noticed that security was at its lowest at dinner times. For the soldiers in the watch towers it was time to change guard. Fifty per cent of the prison staff went for their dinner and only two prison officers were left to open the gates to let the food truck in. The plans were sent through semaphore messages. There were 12 different codes in the semaphore system and we had three semaphorists in each compound who learned each code off by heart. They became so good at sending messages that they could change to a different code half way through messages. The plans were endorsed by Gusty and Jimmy Craig, and now it was a just a matter of when to put the operation into action. We decided on the next Monday.

A joint commando style unit of ten men were selected in each compound and they moved into the hut nearest the compound gates. The one hitch in the plan was that the food lorry delivered to Compound 11 first and then

Compound 12. We needed to delay the prison officers at C11 until the lorry was at C12 so that both compounds would be exposed at the same time. Two men from each compound acted as orderlies and went out to the gates every meal time every day. The orderlies were summoned to a meeting of compound officers and the dilemma was explained. The orderlies related through their routine at every meal time. They checked the food containers to ensure there were enough meals for every prisoner and also that the meals looked properly cooked and in good order. Sometimes there were meals short and they would request the prison officers to check the numbers or complain and then the appropriate action would be taken. If the meals were insufficient in numbers then extra meals would be ordered. The orderlies stated that they could deliberately create a delay through complaining to the prison officers on duty and that should be enough to rectify the hitch. The officers in charge were confident now that they could pull it off.

Monday morning came around and everyone acted as normal. The orderlies went to the gates to get the breakfast and brought the cornflakes and milk churns into the canteen. We had our daily PT and muster parade and then practiced our drill movements. Prisoners were called to visits, and requests to see the doctor, welfare court appearances etc were all carried out as normal. Even the prison officers walked round the inside of the compounds in their token one hour each morning.

Relationships with prison staff were better than any other prison in the UK. If any disturbances broke out, the prison officers withdrew and the British Army riot squads were sent in. This was in one way the best option, as if there was any brutality, then relationships with prison officers were not compromised.

As dinner time approached, prisoners were becoming nervous and anxious but they continued to act in a normal way. Activity in the compound usually reduced as dinner time approached so most of us retired to our huts, only on this day we quickly set about preparing for the takeover. The ten volunteers in the commando unit slipped into the end hut with their make-shift weapons of bed ends and table legs. They donned masks and waited for the order. Both compounds were now ready to implement their plans. Nothing seemed out of place as the food lorry pulled up outside Compound 11. The two orderlies walked towards the gates, pulling the small truck on which they loaded the food from the lorry. As planned, they started to count the number of meals and then called the prison officer to dispute the number. The prison officer began to recount the meals as requested. The food lorry arrived at C12 and the same routine was played out. When the gates of both compounds were open the order was given. Immediately ten men burst out of the huts in each compound and raced to the gates. The two prison officers were taken completely by surprise. They were told they would not be harmed and to leave the area and they duly complied. The compounds, with precision military action, were now in control of the prisoners. Simultaneously UDA members in C11 and the UVF/RHC prisoners in C12 burst out of their huts and lined up in columns of three at the gates with their make-shift weapons. The semaphorists were immediately onto the roof and sending messages. Then the order to march was given and they walked out of the gates and marched by each other into their respective compounds. It took less than ten minutes to complete and now C12 was a UDA compound and C11 was a UVF/RHC. Now it was a waiting game to see how the prison authorities would react. In C19 the prisoners formed up in columns of three and were then given the order to prepare to scale the barb wire fences. They all broke up into groups, placed tables against the compound fences, and threw mattresses onto the barb wire. C19's role was to go to the aid of prisoners in C11 and C12 if they were brutalised.

There was no attempt by the prison authorities to negotiate even though we hadn't harmed any prison officers and we were not running about wrecking things or trying to escape. We knew then that they were taking a hard line and it would only be a matter of time before the British Army would be sent in. There we were standing with our makeshift weapons, no stones or missiles and nowhere to run. This was going to be hand to hand fighting. I'm not saying we were all Bravehearts but our backs were against the wire and we had chosen to stand together and whatever would be would be. Our semaphorist in C11 spotted the first signs of the British Army entering Phase 5 so we knew there was no turning back now. The soldiers marched up to the compound gates in their riot gear, with rubber bullets and CR gas. They were also supported by Saracen armoured cars. At C11 Billy Aiken stood with a steel weightlifting bar. Billy was big and strong and fearless. The OC Jim 'Big O' Irvine also was at the gates. The gates were unlocked so the soldiers were at liberty to enter the compound. Their sergeant gave the order for the snatch squads to enter and they attempted to get in but they hadn't taken into account that they had to get past Billy Aiken, who was swinging the weightlifting bar like an ancient broad sword. Three times we beat them back while their frustrated sergeant was kicking and punching his soldiers to get back in. Having no success with his soldiers he then called up a Saracen armoured car and ordered them to ram the gates. The Saracen backed up a bit then raced towards the inner gate of the compound. The prisoners stood until the very last minute and as the huge armoured car smashed the gates the prisoners moved back to the wire of the compound and stood there waiting for the army to come in. The army duly arrived and there was a Mexican standoff. To be quite honest, I don't think the army knew what to do. We were not throwing missiles, we were not running away; we were standing there ready to fight hand to hand.

The army officer stood there bewildered and the Saracen had come to a halt. Jim 'Big O' Irvine then walked out and spoke to the officer. The only thing the officer was concerned about was our makeshift weapons. Jim Irvine told him we would lay down our weapons under the condition that no one would be brutalised or mistreated. The officer was only too glad to hear that and Jim Irvine warned him that if he broke his word we would fight them with our bare hands. The officer told Jim that he wanted everyone to stand in the search position against the wire fence. Jim Irvine turned to all the men and told them to lay down their weapons and go to the wire. He also told them that if anyone was abused everyone was to get stuck in with the bare hands. The prisoners duly obeyed, except for Jim, who stood and watched every prisoner getting searched before he went to the wire. You never saw a more courteous search by the British Army in your life. The semaphorists remained on top of the huts throughout the riot and were still there. They were told to remain there until we were certain that the Army would not brutalise us. I don't think they were even searched. When everyone had been searched and the Army were satisfied that things were under control, the officer reported to the prison authorities. A short time later, senior prison officers arrived at the compounds. Their main concern was to get everybody back to their proper compounds, and check that no one had escaped, then lock us up and deal with anything else in the morning. The prisoners' own officers lined the relevant men up in columns of three and marched back to their assigned compounds as they had been swapped.

CHAPTER 14

Camp Council

GUSTY, WHO HAD been in the Crumlin Prison since 1966, had shared the same wing and landing as Republican prisoners such as Francis Card and Billy McKee, founding members of PIRA, and other senior ranking Official IRA. Although we were housed in separate compounds, Republicans and Loyalists did come in to contact walking to visits, going to doctors, on welfare visits, legal visits and during other aspects of prison life. Most prisoners were raw off the street and there was always a possibility of conflict on these occasions when they came into contact. Gusty approached the commanders of the Official IRA, PIRA, and the UDA about drawing up a no-conflict policy within the camp between the different factions. A quasi-secret meeting was set up by a number of senior prison officers without the knowledge of the Governor as he would have been content for prisoners to fight among themselves every day of the week. The commanders agreed that no matter what happened on the outside, there would be a no-conflict policy within the camp. This was a holding position and there would be a proper agreement sorted later. They also agreed that it would be good to hold regular meetings for mutual benefit and the seeds of a Camp Council were sown.

The prison regime refused to recognise the Camp Council officially and the Governor was at pains to point this out. He was the boss and no-one else. The Camp Council continued to meet in semi-secrecy whilst frontline prison staff provided a cover of the Prison Welfare Office as a meeting place. At first no records of the meetings were taken but as confidence and trust grew between the factions it was agreed that future meetings would be recorded and that everyone would get a copy. If the Governor had known the meetings were taking place he probably would have nuked the place.

Unity of purpose within prison among prisoners is a mighty weapon. It is better to act together and the situation we were in at the time left us with no other choice or we would have been consumed by a ruthless and determined regime. The Camp Council became impatient and angry with the attitude of the prison authorities refusing to officially recognise their negotiating rights. We needed to do something collectively to demonstrate that we would act together whenever we felt that it was the best way to improve prison conditions. The Camp Council drew up a list of over 30 grievances and complaints ranging from food quality and quantity, visits to be improved, education, handicraft tools, laundry, medical treatment, structure of administration in prison etc, and sent them to the Governor (see Appendix 3). He refused to meet or recognise the Camp Council.

The Camp Council had been challenged, so now they had to send a strong message to the prison authorities. It was done in a simple way. Every Nissen hut had an emergency bell on the inside which was connected to an emergency light on the outside that flashed whenever the bell was pushed. Through the Camp Council we came up with the strategy that at 12 noon on the following Sunday every bell in every hut in the camp would be pressed and held for 15 minutes. Sunday was the quietest day and also the day when there were the least number of prison officers on duty. The day began just as normal with each compound behaving as they usually did on any Sunday, until 12 noon when all hell broke loose. Something like 80 bells and flashing lights could be heard and seen throughout the whole camp. The prison officers panicked, running into their huts using their phones and panic buttons. The resident Army riot squad was put on stand-by and reinforcements were sent from nearby Lisburn army camp. They were expecting a mass riot or breakout. When the bells stopped and the lights stopped flashing, the prisoners went about as normal. the prison officers stood around like fools and the Army was returned to their base. It did send out a strong message and the Camp Council could no longer be ignored. The Governor tried but the Northern Ireland Office (NIO), embarrassed by the call out of troops and the possibility of a major incident in the camp, overruled him.

The Camp Council had a big influence both inside the prison and politically on the outside. This can be demonstrated by the reproduction of proposals sent to the Prison Governor in November 1976.

To: The Governor, Long Kesh, HMP Maze

17th November 1976

It is proposed by the five under mentioned persons that a series of discussions involving them be permitted to take place in the prison study hut. In order to ensure security is not endangered or contravened it is further proposed that an Assistant Governor or Chief Officer be present during such discussions. A cursory glance at the subjects for debate and the persons advocating them will have a strong bearing on whether permission is granted or denied. We can truly state that nothing but good can stem from such a seminar more especially since all the participants espouse two diametrically opposed causes with each individual group having subtle differences on a main theme. This proposition is quite and strictly within the bounds of an educational programme and we feel that the subject matter is very pertinent to life in Ulster today and perhaps tomorrow.

CO Provisional IRA

CO Ulster Defence Association

CO Ulster Volunteer Force/Red Hand Commando

CO Irish Repub Soc Party

CO 'Official' IRA

Subjects for debate

An Independent Ulster

Violence in our Society

Reconciliation

Prisoners Dependents

Resettlement of Prisoners

Political Status and its phasing out

Political and Paramilitary Organisations from United Irishman to present day

Britain and Ireland, Britain and the Irish Republic

Growing Nationalism in the UK

The Irish Constitution

The role of minorities in the Republic's Affairs

Socialism and the paramilitaries

The churches' role in Ireland, North and South

Community Development

Culture and Art in Ireland

A study of co-operative enterprises

To think that the leaders of the paramilitaries inside Long Kesh were so progressive in their thinking in 1976 is absolutely mind blowing.

The Camp Council entered into negotiations with the Northern Ireland Office about setting up an office in downtown Belfast for all political prisoners. All factions would be represented and the office would be funded by the government and would address issues such as reintegration of prisoners and reconciliation. The office would be staffed by ex-political prisoners of all factions, programmes and projects would be geared to bringing about peace and a political agreement that everyone could live with. These groundbreaking proposals where far ahead of the times but the NIO knew very well the potential good and influence that the prisoner population could bring to the whole situation in Northern Ireland. Talks with the NIO were going well in the early stages, but the ending of Special Category Status, the dirty protest and the eventual killing of prison officers led the NIO to postpone the negotiations. They were never resumed, and it was another missed opportunity to move in the right direction and bring the war to an end.

CHAPTER 15

The Ho Chi Min Trail

ONE THING YOU could be sure of was that a protest in Long Kesh was never far away. The most protested issue was the food. It was often cold, undercooked or insufficient. The layout and size of the prison camp was mostly to blame. It was a sprawling 26 acre site and the cookhouse had originally been built to cater for internees, only now it was catering for sentenced prisoners, remands and internees. The food truck was loaded up at the gatehouse with containers relating to each compound. Numbers etc were supposed to be correct and then they set off on their tour of the Kesh. Therefore, if you happened to be among the last of the compounds, your food was often cold and there was no means of heating it up. Quite often the number of meals would be short and we would have to reorder more food, which took maybe an hour or more to arrive. Sometimes they couldn't provide the same meal and some prisoners would go without.

Prisoners were allowed one food parcel per week and often teamed up with fellow prisoners to share throughout the week. The prison tuck shop was another avenue to supplement your rations although there was not much of a variety and the prices were extortionate.

How do you rectify these issues from inside the prison? Many representations were made by all factions to the prison authorities about the quality and quantity of food but to no avail. No matter how many times we complained, they never seemed to do anything. Either they couldn't improve the service or they didn't want to. Such was the frustration that we started to refuse our dinners. When the truck arrived with the food our orderlies had the authority to refuse the meals if they were not up to an acceptable standard and also if they were short in numbers.

Tensions were rising and the prison authorities remained stoic and unconcerned. This tension was exacerbated when the Governor closed access to the prison shop for all prisoners who were involved in the protest. The move was raising the stakes and angered prisoners even more. Finally after three days of returning unacceptable food back to prison officers, frustrations got the better of us. We escalated the protest by including another long drawn out grievance – that of prison laundry. Sheets and pillowcases were supposed to be laundered every fortnight but more often than not it had reduced to a monthly change of laundry. We gathered our sheets and pillow cases and any other items of laundry and festooned them on the barb wire fences like decorations. It was bizarre but it reflected the anger of the prisoners towards the prison regime. The prison retaliated by announcing that they would stop all food parcels to prisoners who were involved in the protest. In effect they were now trying to starve us into submission. We had very little supplies left so it was back to the drawing board to see what, if any, options we had. This went on for about a week and there was no response from the prison authorities.

Finally, frustrations exploded and we threw the food along with their containers over the wire and unto the road that divided the compounds. From then on, every day, twice a day, food prepared in the camp cookhouse met the same fate. Different prisoners took it in turns to have the pleasure of catapulting the food containers over the wretched wire, so that the prison could not isolate or punish any single individuals. We continued to negotiate with the prison regime and they continued to sit on their hands.

The strangest of things then developed, as we thought that starvation or violence was the only means of bringing this protest to an end. We were one Loyalist compound surrounded by five Republican compounds. We were in C19 and the next day we got a call from Republicans in C20. Republican internees who were not involved in the dispute and had access to an abundance of food and parcels offered to feed us. That seemed a nice gesture but they were at the other end of the camp. The Camp Council then had an emergency meeting and a pulley system was suggested where we could haul the food from compound to compound and supply us with enough food to keep the protest going.

The camp was now draped in a makeshift system. Sheets were cut up and weaved together to substitute as ropes. Broken chair legs were twisted and turned to make grappling hooks and the ropes were attached. Prisoners, both Loyalists and Republicans, took to the roofs of the huts where they cast their homemade pulleys to each other. Pillow cases stuffed with all sorts of food were then attached to the pulley and then pulled across the space between each compound. The sight was one to behold as pillowcases full of food were trailed from compound to compound throughout the whole camp. It took hours but eventually every compound in the camp was now stocked up with food. The Vietnam War was in full flow then so we dubbed it the 'Ho Chi Min Trail'. The prison officials looked on in amazement, powerless as this food line bobbled its way around the whole camp. The collective action and cooperation of the Camp Council had reduced the prison regime to spectators.

CHAPTER 16

The Fire

MUCH HAS BEEN written about the burning of Long Kesh by Republican prisoners in October 1974, but nothing from a Loyalist perspective. There were just over 300 Loyalists, sentenced prisoners, remand prisoners and internees. We were spread out all over the camp intermittently between Republican compounds. We were in C9, C11, C12, C14 and C19, while about 1200 Republican prisoners occupied the rest of the compounds. We had a no conflict policy, which had been honoured by all factions from its introduction in 1973 by the Camp Council.

On this day I was walking around the Compound 19 yard with a comrade and everything seemed normal. We were sandwiched between compounds 16, 17, 18 and 20 which held PIRA prisoners, and 21, which held Official IRA prisoners. Since I had obtained the Fáinne Glas in Irish (see Chapter 19) they would usually stop talking as I was walking by. This time they didn't which made me listen more intently to what they were saying. We slowed down our pace and when they had finished their conversation I noticed Republican prisoners rushing about in all their compounds. I hurried over to the hut where Gusty's cubicle was and he was sitting on his bed enjoying a smoke of his pipe. I told him that the Provos were going to burn the camp and he said to me "have you got the proper translation?" I assured him I had.

He got up off his bed and walked over to the wire facing Compound 16 where the OC of the PIRA prisoners, David Morely, was based. He shouted across the wire to a Republican prisoner to tell David Morely he wanted to speak to him. Morely duly appeared at the wire and explained to Gusty that there had been an incident in Compound 13 between prison officers and four prisoners and the prison authorities were refusing to allow him, as Commanding Officer, to go down to Compound 13 and address the situation.

Due to size of the camp and the number of compounds there was an agreement between the Camp Council and the prison that if there were any incidents in the compounds the OC of the faction involved could travel to the compound involved with a view to resolving the incident. On this occasion the prison refused David Morely permission to leave his own C17 and travel about a thousand yards to C13 where the incident happened. Morely warned the camp authorities that if the army were sent in they would resist to the point of "burning the camp to the ground".

Gusty ordered the semaphorist into the hut to make contact with C9, C11, C12 and C14. C11 and C12 were about 700 yards away, C14 was about 500 yards, while C9 was the farthest at about 1500 yards. In minutes semaphore flags were waving out their messages between the compounds. We quickly got an summary of what had happened.

In C13 four masked Republican prisoners, armed with batons, had attacked two prison officers during their routine walk around the compound. They then fled back into their huts. The prison officers retired from C13 and the Governor demanded that the CO of C13 hand over the four attackers. He refused to do so and then demanded that the OC of the PIRA, Morely, be brought from C16 to resolve the situation. The Governor refused, so now there was a Mexican stand-off. We believed then that the incident had been engineered in order to bring about this situation, so we were concerned about where it would all end. More men were dispatched to the hut roofs to act as look outs. It was a massive camp now, with 21 compounds spread over acres of land, us Loyalists only occupying five of them. The Camp Council's 'no conflict' policy had stood for almost two years but in this situation we were uncertain.

Tensions rose as the stand-off continued. The semaphores were immensely useful for getting information. C9 was the nearest to the front gates and the Republican internee compounds. They were also in the greatest danger. We were then told to make weapons to protect ourselves should the need arise. However, C19 was surrounded by five Republican compounds so I don't think we would have stood a chance. The prison officers were still in the camp and patrolling the perimeter of the compounds. We took it that somewhere negotiations were taking place to defuse the situation and hoped that those negotiations would be successful.

Then we got the first indication that any negotiations that were taking place had failed. The prison officers left the whole area and also left us in the shit. We immediately took over the compound with UVF, RHC and UDA all working together. We had wire clippers secreted in a hide and quickly put them to use, cutting a number of holes in the fences leading to the rear of the camp. Mattresses were used to throw over the barb wire and a squad of Loyalists climbed over and secured the doubled gated entrance to our compound. The rest of the Loyalists were put on parade in the centre of the compound in ranks of three. At that point it was not clear whether we were going to survive the night. I looked behind me and about 300 yards away the same prison officers were now standing with armed British Soldiers at the outer perimeter, just looking on as the situation developed. It was very evident that they were not going to lift a finger to help us. Republican prisoners in C16, C17, C18, C20 and C21 lined up in columns of three and were clearly armed with all sorts of make-shift weapons.

We started to get semaphore messages from C9 saying that fighting had begun at the front of the camp between Republican internees and the army. The internees had set fire to their own compounds, the prison cookhouse, kitchens and administration buildings. The Army were firing rubber bullets and tear gas, and beating the internees back up the camp. Gusty immediately gave the order to prepare to evacuate. Compounds 11 and 12 were also ordered to prepare for evacuation. With darkness descending the semaphore system would become useless, so the semaphorists remained on the roof to observe along with other look outs. Gusty, OC of UVF/RHC and Jimmy Craig, OC of the UDA, then went to the wire to talk to Morely, OC of the PIRA prisoners. Morely gave them assurances that our compounds would not be attacked or burned and he was prepared to place Republicans as sentries to prevent any such attacks. Gusty explained that he was more worried about C11, C12 and C9, who were in the middle of the riot and were in possible danger. He told Morely he had made a decision to evacuate C9, C11 and C12 and bring all our volunteers up to C19 and C14, away from immediate danger. He told Morely he was sending Ronnie McCullough and Robert Bates down to Phase 5, where the compounds were, to deliver the orders, and wanted safe passage assured for all Loyalists. Morely granted that request and stationed four Republican prisoners outside our compound gates as a sign of security.

Republican prisoners were now pouring out of their compounds onto the road between. They lined up in columns of three facing towards the football fields at the centre of the camp. Ronnie McCullough and Robert Bates ran past them, heading to C9 first. Not a word was said to them as they passed hundreds of Republican prisoners armed with make-shift weapons. They ran to C9, where the fighting was only 100 yards away. There were about 30 Loyalist remand prisoners waiting there, carrying whatever personal possessions they could grab, and they headed up to C11 and C12. They marched in columns of three past hundreds of Republican prisoners also in columns of three and not a word was spoken. They explained that their compound had been invaded by hundreds of Republican internees and they thought they were goners. However, when they explained they were Loyalists the internees then left the compound.

They arrived at C11 and C12, where about 180 Loyalist prisoners were standing in columns of three with their few possessions, ready to move up to C19. They were led by OC Jim Irvine (C11) and John McKeague (C12). The OCs not only told them to line up in columns of three but also to put their UVF/RHC uniforms on as well. UDA Prisoners were split between the football fields where they joined our ranks. The remainder had already gone to the Loyalist Internee Compound 14. That made a grand total of 212 Loyalists lined up in columns of three preparing to enter the football fields. In the football fields there were about 800 Republican prisoners preparing to join the fight with the Republican internees against the British Army. No one could predict what was going to happen.

All the COs and NCOs Jim Irvine, John McKeague, Ronnie McCullough, and Trevor King stood beside the men in the corridor up the centre of the football fields. They gave the order to march to the Loyalists, telling them to keep their eyes straight ahead and proceed to the gate that would lead them up to the entrance and into Phase 6 and C19. Prisoners told me it was surreal as they marched past the armed PIRA prisoners, and not a word was said or a gesture shown. The noise of the riot was drowned in the silence of the moment. We were waiting on the other side and were relieved as the last row of prisoners, flanked by their officers, came through the gate leading into our compound. When researching this book and talking to prisoners about that moment, most thought they would be killed.

Looking back now I can only point to the work of the Camp Council and the discipline of the prisoners as to why that situation did not deteriorate into a wholesale sectarian massacre. Maybe some would have liked that. The elation of coming together with our other comrades was a relief; at least we were all together. The only blemish of the night was after we had evacuated C9, C11, and C19, some Republicans failed to live up to their word and set fire to the vacant Loyalists compounds, destroying our personal possessions. We learned later, that a short time after we had evacuated the compound's, Terence 'Cleeky' Clarke led a crowd of Republican prisoners into our compounds and set them alight. However, we did not dwell on it and were grateful that we were all, so far as it went, safe and alive.

The practical side effects of the move created further problems, as we now had over 300 prisoners in the one compound. We worked out what we could manage and the rest went down to C14. We removed all the beds from the huts and put the mattresses on the floor to create more space but there would not be much sleeping that night. The hut electricity and the water was off, so we stood outside our huts watching the riots unfold. At around 4.00 am there was lull in the fighting. The Republicans had been pushed back and were all gathered in the football fields.

Some of us nipped back into the hut for a short nap. The Phase 6 medical hut was just across from our compound, and a squad of prisoners raided the site and took bandages, plasters, cotton wool and anything we thought would be useful, including two prison officer uniforms. A few helicopters were in the air, swooping over the camp with their huge long beams of light. Gusty tried to make contact with someone in authority, by shouting to some prison officers and soldiers over the perimeter at the back of the camp but he got no response. The Army seemed content that with the perimeter secured and the Republicans corralled in the football fields they would wait for dawn, so we settled down in the huts playing cards, chatting to each other and waiting for morning to arrive.

When dawn broke through, the activity of helicopters increased tenfold over the camp. I don't how many choppers there were but it was the most I had seen in the air at the same time. I went and looked out at remains of the PIRA compounds, which were completely burned to the ground. I then climbed onto the roof of the hut and viewed the smouldering ashes of the whole camp. The only things left standing was C19 and C14. I could see movement in the football fields and we prepared for whatever was to come. Semaphores between C14 and C19 were operating again and as we approached 9.00 am the battle began anew. The helicopters began to drop what we thought was CS gas but turned out to be a more potent form of gas called CR. They just hovered over the football fields dropping the canisters at will. C14 had a better view and they were able to keep us posted through the semaphore system. They informed us that more troop reinforcements were piling into the camp and now had it surrounded. They could also see more troops waiting on the outside. The gas was everywhere, spreading into our own compounds and affecting our men. The situation was hopeless. The introduction of helicopters, gas and massive reinforcements meant the battle was virtually over. A prison riot is completely different from a street riot – you have nowhere to run.

Republicans began moving their injured out of the football fields back into Phase 6, just outside our compound. We used the wire clippers to cut the fences and make entrances into C19. Those who we thought were the most seriously injured we brought into our compound, into the wooden study hut and gave them first aid using the medical supplies we had procured the night before. Gusty continued to try to negotiate through the perimeter wire to bring the riot to an end with the blessing of Morely. Eventually he was able to make contact with someone of authority. It was agreed that all the prisoners would return to their own compounds and the authorities would call off the helicopters to allow them to do so. This was relayed to Morely who agreed and ordered the Republicans back to their compounds. The helicopters hovered in the distance but stopped dropping the CR gas canisters. When all the prisoners had returned to their compounds, the Army moved in. We were the only compound left standing in Phase 6 but that didn't stop the army moving into our compound too. It was quite obvious that they were not aware of the nuances of the camp, the fact we were Loyalists and that we were not involved in the riot. Gusty immediately formed us into columns of three and brought us to attention. This brought a moment of astonishment from the soldier's Sergeant who didn't know what to do. Gusty then marched forward and spoke to the Sergeant of the riot troops. You could see the bewilderment on the face of the Sergeant. He thought for a moment and then told Gusty to get us all into our huts. Gusty spun round in military fashion, gave the order to dismiss and moved all of us into the canteen so that we would remain together. As we made our way into the canteen hut we could see the Republicans being thrown against the wire and roughly treated. The brutality at that point was not by the soldiers that had been involved in the riot, but by those who had relieved them. The soldiers commandeered the study hut and told us we would have to go into the hut and be searched and photographed, and to give our names. However, we had retrieved our security books with our photos and details from the prison officers hut the night before and had held them intact. Gusty asked to speak to the Sergeant in charge and informed him that we had all the security books intact and then went into his hut and brought out the tray with all our books in it. The sergeant then said that we would only be searched and checked against the security books. One by one we entered the study hut, were searched and any contraband such, as money etc was confiscated. As I walked from the canteen to the study hut I looked over at the Republican compounds and could see that they were all still against the wire. Some were being mistreated but nothing compared to what would eventually happen. I walked into the hut to get searched. I noticed these soldiers were wearing red berets and later learned that they were attached to the parachute regiment. So of all the soldiers to have in our compound, we got the Para's. The soldier who was searching me was about 7ft tall and built like the side of a house. I remember straining my neck up to look at him and thinking to myself thank god we didn't have to fight you lot. I had money hidden in my mouth but they asked me my name and I couldn't answer so they discovered it and I returned to the canteen penniless.

The camp was now under control of the Army and at about 2.00 pm fresh troops arrived to relieve those soldiers who had been involved in the riot. That's when the brutality began in earnest. We were all locked in the canteen and could only view C20 through the small windows of the hut. The troops who took over immediately began to brutalise the prisoners, making them run a gauntlet of batons and then throwing them against the wire fences. I had never seen such brutality in all my life. It stopped for a while and food trucks appeared. We were given loaves of bread and blobs of margarine and a pint of milk each. The bread worked out at exactly two rounds each. They then delivered to C20 and the soldiers put the bread in the centre of the compound. They placed each prisoner's two rounds of bread and pint of milk on the ground, and then tramped and spat on the bread. Republicans couldn't see this as they were faced against the fence. They then turned the prisoners round one by one and made them run a gauntlet of batons to get their food. It was disgusting to watch. After about ten prisoners, they turned the next prisoner around and he refused to run the gauntlet. I don't know who he was but they hit him repeatedly with batons and he defiantly refused to move. The soldiers knew now knew that they had gone too far and so for the rest of the prisoners they just made them run without the gauntlet. About five minutes later an army officer walked over to C20 and spoke to the Sergeant in charge. I don't know what he said to him but there was no more brutality.

At about 5.00 pm the army withdrew from the compounds but remained in charge of the camp. They carried out routine foot patrols on the road between the compounds. We were anxious to contact the prison authorities to connect with some sort of civilian authority. That contact didn't come until later in the evening.

In the mayhem of the riot and fire we found out later that six Loyalist internees had broken out of Compound 14 and passed hundreds of Republicans to rescue a Loyalist prisoner from the prison hospital. When they arrived at the hospital the prison officers had abandoned the sick prisoners to their fate. The rescue party shouted out "any Loyalists here?" and were made aware of one Loyalist prisoner. They told him of the situation and that they were there to take him to the safety of Compound 14. A prisoner in the next bed to him identified himself as a member of the Official IRA and requested the rescue party take him to Compound 14 also. The raiding party warmly accepted his request and accompanied both prisoners back through the riot to the safety of Compound 14.

CHAPTER 17

The Aftermath

WE HAD LOST contact with the outside world and they with us. Rumours abounded causing widespread violence in both Loyalist and Republican areas. In Loyalist areas rumours were rife that we had been attacked by Republicans and many of us had been killed. In Republican areas there were rumours that the army had killed many prisoners. Of course the NIO couldn't confirm or deny anything because the Prison Service had abandoned us all to whatever fate that would befall us. All the outside world could see was the flames of the camp lighting up the October sky. We were concerned about our families and our families about us. The lack of communication fed the rumours. The uncertainty created speculation in the media and furore in the streets and the political world. Worried families, who could, made their way to Long Kesh but were halted by a ring of steel around the perimeter of the camp.

The next morning I got up onto the roof of the hut to survey the damage. It was a scene of devastation and suffering. The only buildings left standing were Compounds 14 and 19. The rest of the camp was left a crumbled and smouldering mass of tangled corrugated tin sheeting. The prison authorities were completely disorganised and there was a humanitarian crisis on their hands. We were seriously overcrowded, with 250 prisoners crammed into accommodation made for 90. We had seven or eight prisoners wedged into cubicles made for two prisoners; were sleeping on the floor on mattresses; and had no heat and no running water. It was a nightmare and there was no quick remedy for this situation. However, no matter how much we were suffering, Republicans were in a far worst situation.

Republicans had been forced to make lean-to shanty huts out of tangled corrugated sheets and debris, which they placed against the wire fences to give them some shelter. During the night a passing army foot patrol kicked and battered the compound wire and the temporary shelters collapsed on top of the prisoners. There was nothing much the Republicans could do except rebuild their shelters. Every night for the next week the passing foot patrols would kick the temporary shelters and Republicans would rebuild them. Finally, Republicans had had enough and warned the army through the prison authorities that if they did it again Republicans would come over the wire and attack them. The harassment ceased. We then heard that as well as C14 and C19 surviving the fire, Republicans had been selective enough to leave the visiting area intact. This gave us a slender hope that visits would resume earlier than we had anticipated.

Soon the food trucks arrived and just like the day before there were two rounds bread, a blob of margarine and a pint of milk. Gusty and the OC of the UDA met with the prison Governor with long list of complaints and requests. These included that we had about 250 prisoners in a compound built for 90. We had 90 mattresses between 250 prisoners; no electricity; no food except two rounds of bread; and no eating utensils. The prison needed to publicly state that prisoners were safe; visits needed to be resumed as quickly as possible; and there needed to be visits from churchmen and political representatives etc. The Governor explained that the kitchens had been destroyed but they were now going to use army field kitchens to feed us. The food would be delivered by the army and we could distribute it. Other than that we didn't get much more. We also requested that two prisoners, one from C11 and one from C12, be escorted to the relevant compounds to see if there was anything to salvage. This request was granted. Prisoners from the relevant compounds left with prison officers holding the faint hope that some personal passions could be salvaged. Prisoners from C11, C12 and C9 waited in subdued anticipation. When the prisoners returned from their quest they reported that there was nothing that could be salvaged as the compounds and the contents had been virtually incinerated. We were angry! We were angry that Republicans had broken their word. We were angry that a lot of personal contents had been destroyed, but in the whole round of things I suppose we were grateful we weren't in the huts when they were set on fire. We accepted the loss and got on with trying to improve our conditions.

The Army field kitchens arrived in the afternoon and unloaded their trucks with what looked like ammunition boxes with the food inside. Our appointed orderlies set up a table. Paper plates and plastic utensils were provided. When they opened the ammunition boxes a wave of steam rose from them – it looked like stew but we could smell the acrid stench of diesel. We began to eat the meal, and some of us threw up at the taste of the diesel, while some of us refused to touch it and there were the proverbial few who were asking for seconds. This definitely would not be acceptable. We immediately sent for senior prison officers and told them that the food was unacceptable and we demanded proper meals. The camp was in a mess and the authorities were not in a hurry to fix it.

While we were living in these torrid conditions, protests and pressure was being exerted from the outside but in the inside we could see no hurried movement. The whole infrastructure of the prison had been destroyed. Unionist politicians and their supporters showed no sympathy for the prisoners, because as far as they were concerned the prisoners burned the camp and it was their own fault that they were in the present position. Only our families, supporters and a few independent Unionists expressed any concern for our plight. Unrest and anger was now building up throughout all factions among the prison population.

The overcrowding, poor sanitary conditions and kitchen facilities were totally inadequate. Toilets were blocked up, raw sewage flowed in the ablutions and we had one gas ring for cooking between 180 men. It was now November, edging into December, and there was no sign of any movement to redress the situation. The prisoners were now threatening a hunger strike. Although we were promised a rebuilding programme immediately after the fire, it appeared that the authorities were dragging their feet. Twelve volunteers started a hunger strike to highlight the plight of the men behind the wire, and more and more political pressure and protests were haemorrhaging on the outside. Bomb scares and hijackings were a daily occurrence. We could see from our roofs that work had started to rebuild Phase 5 of the Camp containing C9, C10, C11, C12 and C13. The COs of each of the factions were taken on a visit to the Phase 5 rebuilding programme to see for themselves how work was progressing. They were assured that prisoners would be in these compounds within two weeks. They left with these assurances and the hunger strike, hijackings and protests were suspended on the basis that we would be in these reconstructed compounds within the fortnight. The days dragged by as we kept looking from our vantage positions on the roofs of our huts to see how the rebuilding programme was progressing. Sometimes it would seem as if nothing was happening and then a hut would spring up all of a sudden. We began counting the number of huts that went up each day and longing to get back to some kind of normality. The greatest danger we had in the immediate term was that many prisoners were starting to fall victim to the flu. There was a very real threat that this could turn into an epidemic and spread throughout the whole camp. Doctors were forewarned of the problem and more medicines and precautions were taken to try to prevent the spread of influenza.

On the 7 December prisoners were moved from the burnt out Phase 6 back down to the reconstructed compounds in Phase 5 and into Compound 13. We were never as glad to see new bedding, bedclothes and the luxury of having a warm shower. These new huts were certainly thrown up quickly and shabbily, as there were draughts, disjointed doors and windows, and the brick gable ends were substituted with large sheets of wood. However, it was better than the conditions we had endured for the past 54 days. Now we could settle down for the Christmas period and build up our personal belongings and contraband again. Slowly but surely as the days went by we were getting used to these temporary huts, even though they were freezing.

About a week before Christmas I was tucked up in my bed with my plastic bottle filled with hot water warming my bed and my feet. The winter winds were howling outside and as I was about to doze over, there was the almightiest thud and the whole hut shook. I almost jumped out of my bed. It was like an earthquake and as I sat up the mightiest wintry wind blew up the hut, blowing everything all over the place. Still unsure of what had happened, I looked down the hut and could see the outside wire fence and the stars in the sky. The wooden gable end had blown down and was now lying in the compound yard.

CHAPTER 18

Security before Humanity

THE MENTION OF a prison hospital gave the public the perception that somehow dedicated medical staff and care was available for those incarcerated in the various prisons, prison camps and prison ships throughout the country. However, the experience of prison medical care was rather different. When it came to a tossup between humanity and security, security always won.

In the Long Kesh wilderness, if you took seriously ill there was a long list of security checks before you could be taken to hospital or even to see a doctor, especially at night. In each Nissen hut there was an 'emergency' bell attached to a long steel pole on the outside with an emergency red light that flashed like an ambulance. If someone was unwell and prisoners pressed the bell the compound prison officers would enter the compound after clearance from security. They would ascertain what the problem was without opening the doors and then contact the duty Medical Orderly (MO) who would, again after security clearance, enter the compound. A riot squad would be put on standby and then on clearance by security they would enter the hut. The MO would look at the patient and on his assessment it would be decided whether a prisoner would be sent to an outside hospital. This would entail security contacting the RUC to provide an escort to the hospital, and the waiting time would depend on manpower and availability. A hospital would also have to be contacted for availability. Security clearance would have to be given before any prisoner, no matter how ill they were, could leave the compound and head for an outside hospital. This whole operation could take up to six hours or more.

I was in Compound 12 in 1973 when Hugh Arnold McClean took ill at about 10.00 pm after lock up. He had been in Musgrave Park Hospital (Prison Wing) for a period but they had returned him back to the prison a few weeks before. In the open Nissen hut housing 30 other prisoners, Hugh was evidently seriously ill, for us all to see. He had been ill for some time but despite numerous visits to the prison doctor, he was not deemed ill enough to be treated in an outside hospital. We pressed the 'emergency' bell and it took about 20 minutes for a prison officer to come to our window. He shouted in at us asking what was the emergency? We shouted back with urgent words explaining the seriousness of the situation but he just turned complacently and said he would inform security. A couple of prisoners were attending to Hugh's needs as much as they possibly could but in the environment of an open hut Hugh had no privacy whatsoever. The rest of us lay on top of our beds and looked on helplessly. An hour had passed by now and we pressed the emergency bell again for about ten minutes but no one came. I sat on top of my bed opposite Hugh and could hear him struggle for breath. You hear a pin drop in the hut as we stared endlessly at Hugh fighting for his life but we were helpless.

It was about an hour and a half before a naive MO came into the hut, accompanied by prison officers, but they were too late. The hut was vapourised with the odour that one would smell in a funeral parlour, the odour of death. This was the first of many such instances. Dickey Richardson was being treated for six months in the prison camp for 'piles' before a visit to an outside hospital diagnosed him as being afflicted with stomach cancer. He died shortly after his release. Robert Cardwell was in constant pain, particularly in his legs, and was forever complaining to the prison doctor about his ailment. Despite his obvious discomfort the most the medical officer would do was give him a few painkillers. Upon his release he was diagnosed with MS and died shortly afterwards. In those early days the prisoners had no confidence in either the medical or the ethical approach of the prison authorities and prison nursing staff.

In July 1976, Gusty Spence wrote a letter of complaint to the prison doctor in Long Kesh about his concerns regarding the treatment of prisoners in Musgrave Park Hospital prison Wing.

Dear Dr Turner,

Because of the many varied and numerous complaints emanating from Loyalist Prisoners I am forced somewhat reluctantly to bring to your attention certain conditions now prevailing in ward eighteen (security ward) of Musgrave Park Hospital.

I am only too aware that there are prisoners who for different reasons would be malicious in levelling such complaints but I wish to assure you that I have personally investigated the allegations and unfortunately find an element of truth in them, also you will recall, I had occasion to spend two periods in ward eighteen because of illness and can to some degree state with some authority the situation as I saw it. Therefore I am not unacquainted with most of the personnel and general outlay.

As recent records will prove a number of Loyalist Prisoners have taken the quite unusual step of signing themselves out of this ward claiming the expected 'professionalism' existent in a normal hospital does not prevail in this ward, which in fact, has been instituted solely for the purpose of facilitating prisoners.

The general opinion is that within ward eighteen a man is a prisoner first and a patient second which to my way of thinking is not the function or thought of someone pursuing a vocation.

Security must be paramount as far as the security forces are concerned with which no one can possibly take exception because there has been security breaches in this particular ward in the past and at this juncture I wish to make it absolutely clear that there are no objections to any aspect of the behaviour of the security forces except for undue noise by the personnel on night duty and the isolated cases of verbal altercations. It must also be stated that only the highest praise is due to Dr Hall and the other attendant doctors for their concern for humanity as well as their expertise.

The complaints are levelled at the nursing and cleaning staff of whom it is suggested leave much to be desired in carrying out the spirit and tone of their vocation. There is a gross lack of supervision of cleanliness of the various rooms incorporated within ward eighteen and the expected standard of hygiene is not maintained comparable with that in other parts of the hospital. Genuine requests made to the nursing staff are treated in an offhand and sceptical manner and one is labelled a troublemaker if one insists that standards be adhered to and invariably one is removed to a little side ward to dissuade him from his 'insistence'. Mr Mawhinney quite recently made four requests to see a doctor because of his chest pains whilst in ward eighteen and it was only the insistence of other prisoner patients that a doctor was summoned by the nurse. The doctor ordered Mr Mawhinney immediately to Belfast City Hospital because of his heart condition. There were repercussions concerning the prisoner who demanded attention for Mr Mawhinney and these prisoner patients felt obliged to discharge themselves from the custody of ward eighteen back to Long Kesh.

As in all aspects of human relationships there are personality clashes but these clashes appear to be more pronounced between the civil and military forces on duty within ward eighteen and as a result there is an overspill in which the prisoner patient is on the receiving end. I hesitate to mention the nursing staff but reluctantly believe that their permanency in this ward has definitely had a detrimental effect on their efficiency and rotation could be an answer. In so complex a matter it is hard to be specific and obviously this epistle could be treated with reserve but one must ask why so many men are discharging themselves from this ward and returning to Long Kesh. There must be a certain deterrence within all hospitals and indeed the patient must be actively encouraged to recovery but I suggest the 'encouragement' in ward eighteen of Musgrave Park Hospital is too repressive and in many cases undeserved.

It would be that the situation could be monitored discreetly and changes made where required. I think this is a reasonably and logically desirable. Nothing else I believe is necessary.

I conclude by forthrightly stating that I have a reputation for being honest, sensible and responsible. Subsequent inquiries will substantiate what I have stated in this document and if anyone so desires they can question at length any of the prisoners who have discharged themselves of late. I expect that the claims will be contested in certain quarters but I contend that emotionalism and partiality aside, the claims will be admitted.

Thank you for your attention and humanity,

Most Sincerely,
AA Spence

Tommy Mawhinney died in Belfast City Hospital shortly after his transfer from Ward 18 Musgrave Park Hospital.

CHAPTER 19

The Battle for Education

TIME WAS OUR biggest enemy in this POW camp environment and how we used that time was uppermost in Gusty's mind. He told us that prison would either make us or break us; that we would either emerge as bitter men or better men. He was determined that most of us would leave the camp as better men. The challenge to stimulate prisoners' minds in such a harsh and hostile place with so many distractions and impediments was of Everest proportions. The authorities at that time were not interested in providing prisoners with any sort of education or help. They were only interested in locking us up and making sure we didn't escape. If they could've avoided feeding us they would have obliged.

At first we had to develop our own system with our own capabilities at the time. Weapons classes were the simplest to start with as there were plenty of experts among us. Bomb making classes were quickly added, accompanied with informative diagrams and instructions. Replica weapons were made with wood, chair legs, leather, plastic and even bars of soap, and anything else we could use. Some of the weapons were very realistic and could be mistaken for the actual thing. One weapon that was made was a work of art. It was a British Army regulation SLR (7/62) calibre rifle and we would get photos taken posing with it in our hands. It was eventually discovered in a search and now sits in pride of place in the Prison Officers Museum in Millisle. However, that was not the way Gusty wanted us to go.

Gusty wanted to bring in proper education and requested qualified teachers and lecturers to deliver the lessons in the prison. The prison education officer offered us a course on the card game Bridge and some little old lady came into the compound to teach us. I went to the lesson to observe and as we sat round a table she could hardly hold her cards as her hands were shaking so much. Needless to say that was the end of 'prison courses'.

We started to teach ourselves and Gusty held classes in Irish history and politics, trying to get us think about how we ended up in that place, what we could do to understand the conflict and how we could change it. The classes were well attended and interesting. Most of the men went to state schools where Irish history was not taught and the prisoners found it very interesting and challenging as Gusty revealed aspects of our history that did not match the usual stereotypical Loyalist thinking. The political classes were even more interesting and with the captive audience we had we were able to express our thoughts freely, challenging old myths and traditional no nos. It was a breath of fresh air and many progressive ideas and analyses were aired in that wrinkly tin hut. Indeed it has been accepted by most that the seeds of the Good Friday Agreement were first sown in the debates that were encouraged in a mature atmosphere.

I had obtained a few GCE O levels at school and though I had no experience whatsoever in teaching, Gusty asked me to try to teach English language as correspondence by letter was the next best thing to a visit. Although everyone was literate there was not much to write about in Long Kesh so I tried to help them with their creativity. This English class was voluntary but well attended and the men seemed to enjoy it. They were comfortable with me as teacher because I was one of them and they didn't feel inferior. They could also approach me anytime of the day, as I wasn't going anywhere.

We appointed our own education officers and Gusty demanded better library books and access to teachers. This is reflected in a letter from the Rev AH Butler who was Bishop of Connor in October 1973:

Dear Gusty Spence,

Thank you for your letter of October 4th. When I visited you in the camp, you made two specific complaints to me. The first was that there were not enough suitable books to read, and the second was that there should be a series of lectures or talks by suitably qualified people to give some mental stimulation to the men. I spoke to the Governor on the matter of books, and that courses or lectures were in the process of being arranged. Perhaps you will be good enough to let me know what the situation is on these two matters...

Despite great opposition from the prison authorities and some prison staff, we eventually negotiated to bring in qualified lecturers to stimulate the men's thinking and also to attempt to set up Open University (OU) Correspondence Courses in the camp. We were now in unchartered waters and we looked at the adventure with hope and trepidation.

The first exam I did in Long Kesh was a GCE O Level in Sociology, which I passed. I recommend prison as the best place to study because every aspect and example of social learning was there in front of me. I also decided to try and learn Irish because I had plenty of time to do so and it would be useful in the camp. Our compound (C19) was surrounded by five Republican compounds and the prisoners often used the Irish language to shout across to each other, so that neither the prison officers nor us Loyalists could understand them. After a while we got used to the twang and it never bothered us but when the Republicans were marching in their compounds I started to pick up the words for left turn, right turn about turn etc.

I approached a Republican prisoner who was shouting to another Republican prisoner, in Irish, across the wire from C17 to C18. I shouted over to him and asked had they anyone who taught Irish as I was interested in learning the language. He shouted into the hut of C17 and in a few moments another Republican prisoner appeared at the wire and introduced himself as Daciah Power (Davy Power) from the Short Strand area of Belfast. He explained to me he was a 'tutor' in the Irish language and taught Republican prisoners as they came in off the streets. He agreed to teach me the Irish language though we had to work out practicalities. I requested permission from the Governor to allow me to go into C17 to be taught the language. The Governor refused on the grounds of my safety even though Republicans had given categorical assurances I would be safe and I was prepared to go into C17 under those terms. We eventually came to a compromise where I would be allowed out of my compound to go across the road and sit on one side of the fence while my tutor sat on the other side.

It was the summer and we had the long evenings, so I walked out of Compound 19 at 6.00 pm with a chair and notebook, and sat down beside the wire. On the other side sat Daciah Power in a chair with his books. He explained to me that there were three stages to the examinations, the Green Fáinne, the Blue Fáinne and the Gold Fáinne. The Green was the practical speaking of the language, the Blue would be more the written word and grammar and the Gold would be full fluency in Irish. Then he began teaching the fundamentals of the Irish language. The way that Daciah taught me was simple and practical, and the first lesson lasted about 1½ hours. He gave me my homework, bid me farewell and I lifted my chair and returned to my compound. That night I got stuck into my homework and found I was enjoying it. That would be the routine Monday to Friday, at the same time, with chair and notebook under my arm, I would walk and over to C17 to learn my next lesson.

On the fourth night, Daciah passed a bottle of liquid over to me. I asked him what it was and he replied "uisce beatha", the water of life. In other words, poteen! Being a 'townie' I hadn't a clue about the potency of this stuff. After my lesson I went back to the compound and showed it to Gusty and then we took a sip each then shared it round the hut. The next night I had 1 hour tuition and ½ hour learning how to make a still to make poteen. The rest of that story I'll cover later in the book.

Back to Irish language lessons at the wire and I was learning pretty fast. I never asked Daciah why he was in prison; we never talked politics and he was a good teacher and pleasant person. After four weeks he felt that I was ready to sit my Fáinne Glas. He explained he couldn't adjudicate my exam and he would have to get another Republican. The examination was set for Monday night. I went over to C17 as usual, only there was another person with Daciah. I recognised the person; he was Pontias McArt (Francis Card), a founder member of the Provisionals and an Irish Language Invigilator. I sat down in my chair and he introduced himself and I did the same. The oral exam took about ½ hour and then he informed me that I had passed. I was delighted and so was Daciah. I had achieved a Fáinne Glas plus I had learned how to make and distil poteen in the confines of the camp.

There were six people who put their name forward for the educational courses: Ronnie McCullough (RHC), Brendan Mackin (OIRA), Martin O'Hagan (OIRA), William Bratty (UDA), Harry Black (UDA), and me, William 'Plum' Smith (RHC). PIRA refused to engage with the OU because of some clandestine and obscure political reason. This initiative was unique and very progressive to anything that had gone before. There were two courses offered which were deliberately selected so that they would not be seen as controversial. They were Social Sciences and Humanities, both foundation courses, and I selected Humanities while my comrade Ronnie McCullough selected Social Sciences. The tutor would have access once per month and study huts that were located in a compound between the two football pitches would be used as joint educational facilities. This was a massive step for Loyalists and Republicans sitting down in the same room to be taught jointly by a tutor from the OU. There were no computers or telephones then so 95 per cent of the courses depended on hand written correspondence. The other five per cent was the monthly visits by the tutor.

These visits in themselves proved to be a whole major operation. Firstly the tutor arrived and informed the prison staff, and he was then put through the system. There was no special treatment for tutors; they were just treated the same as visitors. They were searched and then kept waiting. There were six of us spread around three compounds so we were then brought to the study huts. Then and only then was the tutor brought to us. So it took a whole morning just to get us in the same room. I often reflect on the bravery and dedication of those first tutors who paved the way to give us the opportunity to a higher level of education. I wonder how they felt on their first day as they walked through those unwelcoming gates, through the searches, through more gates and more gates and then to enter the same room to teach us 'unrepentant terrorists'.

Our essays were written by hand and there were no copies or means of copying them. They also had to go through the prison censorship office just like an ordinary prisoner's letter, and correspondence was often delayed both from us and the OU. During the fortnightly compound searches, we had to bring all our course work with us and keep an eye on it in case it went amiss or was confiscated. Eventually things started to ease up as the prison authorities began to tentatively accept that the OU was there to stay. However, there was great onus on myself and Ronnie McCullough to succeed, being the first from our compound. We worked round the obstacles laid before us, except for when the Provos burnt the camp just before our exams. The OU was suspended for about four months and when we finally sat our exams, we both passed. We had proven to the naysayers and the prison authorities that prisoners, despite the obstacles, even in the confines of Long Kesh, even Loyalists, were capable of reaching the standards of the OU.

Ironically the first lecturer that entered Long Kesh to teach Loyalists was Miriam Daly who taught at Queens University. She lectured us in Irish history and was well liked by the Loyalist prisoners and created a lot of interest. Sadly, in June 1980 she was shot dead in her home in Andersontown by Loyalists.

We had come a long way from the weapons training and bomb making in the early days of 1972. By 1977 five men had passed their Fáinne Glas in the Irish Language; 16 other men were studying and poised to gain their badges in the coming months; 20 men were studying other languages including Spanish, French and German; and 20 men were now also at various stages of a degree whilst studying with the Open University.

CHAPTER 20

Art, Poetry and Pantomimes

In this troublesome and austere wire mesh environment, hidden talents emerged from within the prisoner population that enhanced our daily lives in many different ways. Art and handicrafts were a popular way to pass the long prison days but getting the materials and tools to work with became a big issue. Paint, leatherwork, modelling, wallets, purses, bags, belts, sewing machines, Stanley knives for cutting and shaping the leather, and small hammers for picture framing all had to have permission from the Governor. Eventually tools were allowed but under the condition that they would not remain in the huts overnight. Prison officers would leave a tool box in the hut and then collect all the tools and remove them from the compound before lockup. This actually proved beneficial in the long run, as it was hard to conceal things in the bare Nissen huts, especially our smuggled in cameras and films. We carved a number of secret compartments in the tool box so that the prison officers were looking after our contraband without ever knowing it.

Freddie Stevenson became our first mural artist to adorn the walls and cubicles of Long Kesh. Initially, Freddie was our compound painter and odd man. He would touch up doors and windows ledges with any type or colour of paint he could get his hands on. He also would sketch photos or countryside scenes on paper with a simple pencil and bring them to life with his careful shading. Freddie was then asked to paint a mural in the hut, which was no mean feat for not only did it test his artistic skills but also his borrowing and bribery assets to get the paint and colours he required.

Freddie set about his task in his usual calm and methodical manner. The toughest part was deciding what the content of the mural would be. There were many ideas and much discussion but in the end we played safe and opted for a map of Northern Ireland and the coat of arms of each county.

Where Freddie got the paint and colours from was amazing and when he couldn't get hold of a colour, he would concoct some magic recipe that would produce the required hue. Everyone was pleased with Freddie's inaugural effort and it certainly brightened the hut up. Of course he couldn't wait to get his next assignment. Ideas flowed thick and fast, and Freddie spent the rest of his sentence adorning the huts of Long Kesh with numerous murals.

Billy McConnell emerged from the prisoner population as another hidden artist. He had served in the Merchant Navy and during his spells at sea he spent his spare time drawing portraits with a plain pencil on paper. He had no formal training but was extremely talented. One day he took a photograph of another prisoner's wife and two children, and sketched them out on an A4 letter page. Shadowing and shading with the pencil and his fingers, the finished product was better than the photograph. This revelation that he could draw such eloquent and detailed portraits from photographs kept him busy for the rest of his sentence, as prisoners lined up for him to use his reproduction skills on their family photos.

While doing research for this book, I went up to see Billy at his home in the Glencairn estate in Belfast. I wasn't sure of his address so I went to an old friend who lived in Glencairn and he was able to point out where Billy's house was. He said to me, "you can't miss it it's the one with two sheds." I parked my car and walked down the path between houses and there it was, with two sheds in the garden. I could see the silhouette of Billy through the plastic shed window and could hear a noise. I shouted over the fence and he came out and greeted me.

I told him what I was trying to do and he was delighted. He brought me into his shed, where he had his tools lined up and a large scaled-down replica of the *Titanic* which he was constructing. He had no work plans, just a picture of the ship and was working out the sizes with a set of callipers. Billy could build or make almost anything with the most basic of tools and the sparest of materials. He reckoned he had sketched hundreds of prisoners' children from photographs during his sentence and found it quite enjoyable. He was now doing oil paintings and brought me into the other shed where he had an oil painting hanging of his five daughters. It was a masterpiece. I really enjoyed talking to him after so long and I think he enjoyed it too.

George Morrow also came out of the shadows to reveal his talents as a unique and creative painter. He began with pencil sketches of contemporary day to day life in the camp, recording history using his skill as an artist. As time went by and the regime relaxed about what prisoners could get sent into the prison, George began to paint on canvas. The first time I saw him painting on canvas he was using a knife to draw. I sat dumbfounded as he used the knife to apply thick layers of paint onto the canvas, spreading it onto the surface and massaging it into shape with adept movement of the wrist. I had heard about this style of painting but to witness it being practised in Long Kesh by a fellow prisoner was surreal. George continues to paint and has established himself as an artist, holding a number of exhibitions around the country.

Other prisoners turned to poetry to express their thoughts and feelings. The poems reflected the environment and situation prisoners and detainees found themselves in. Internee Ken Gibson describes his predicament and the anger of being interned and then detained by an unjust and farcical trial referred to as 'Commissioners Courts' in April 1973.

Interned

Interned, interned, Oh! What a day,
To hear that old Commissioner say,
"Your character's good, personality too,
But still my man, I'll detain you."

The day began like any other,
I was taken to a hut without any bother,
Seated in that hut, was a white haired man,
His false teeth loose and his face dead pan.

The Commissioner sat a desk raised high
As he spoke to me he seemed to cry
I looked at these two quaint old men
And wondered just how long they'd spend
In making up their mind to keep
A lad like me in this Long Kesh heap

They growled and boaked as they sat there
Squirming in their easy chair

A blue curtain covered one small corner
Why it was there I began to wonder
But soon my mind was put at ease
As the Special Branch sat there with knocking knees

A paid informer gave me this news
This man has very militant views
I hear he's an officer in the UVF
Hit him with anything that's left
And so from a drunken paid informer
My fate was sealed from that small corner

So in Long Kesh I must remain
Some say interned some say detained
The informer he's in a prison as well
For his soul is ruled from the depths of hell

Another poem, 'A Salute', written by Ronnie McCullough, describes the UVF/RHC prisoners on parade in Compound 11 in June 1973.

A Salute

Those lads in black all looked smart
As they formed in ranks of three
In Ulster's war they played their part
Though yet they were not free

Long Kesh to them is a barrack square
In which to drill and train
And these young men had been put there
With a number not a name

Then stripped of a name and character too
These lads were not dismayed
As lads like these are very few
And their part they've already played

They're drilling now within a cage
And their movements are confined
But all their names could fill a page
With their courage underlined

How proud we'd be if Ulster knew
The actions of these young men
And ranks they formed each day grew
As the rebels they did bend

We'll salute these lads of the UVF
With young hearts full of pride
For they're the ones in prison left
And these facts we cannot hide

This next poem was written by myself in June 1973.

A Dream

For a stroll around this compound
Went my friend and I
And as we walked we laughed and talked
Of our dreams that night gone by

I told him of my peculiar dream
And we thought of it and joked
And then I listened intensively
As of his dream he spoke

He visioned himself in an aul' armchair
His hair was a silvery grey
And around him sat some little kids
And these strife torn years he portrayed

Well kids he said t'was a long time ago
When I was just a lad

The IRA they bombed and maimed
And things were looking bad

So with my friend some time did spend
To decide what should be done
And we brought together some other young men
And armed ourselves with guns

We heard the cry from Ulster's graves
They brought us to the fore
But we knew that time was running out
Each night we went to war

One summer night in '72
I knew our time had come
When a Republican fell down and bled
He was shot by Orange guns

The three of us stood in the dock
The Judge he looked forlorn
And within a matter of minutes
Ten years of our lives were gone

They took us to Long Kesh to serve our time
And at first the years looked long
But we knew the cause we thought was right
And our loyal hearts were strong

So kids be careful in whatever you do
As the years they roll on by
Make sure your motives are Just and True
For the price you pay is high

In an age before mobile phones, internet, facebook, iphones etc we had
to campaign and protest to be allowed a record player into the compound.
It took months to convince prison authorities that allowing prisoners to

play music of their own choice would actually be a good thing. After much argument and letters to the NIO, they finally gave permission for one record player to be allowed into the compound to be shared among 90 prisoners. We were very much looking forward to this 'groundbreaking' move of liberalism by the prison regime, even though we had to buy it ourselves. Prisoners began to send messages out to their family to bring up their private record collections on their next visit. When the day came for the record player to be delivered, about 30 prisoners were queued up outside the study hut where the final resting place of the record player had been agreed. A book was set at the entrance so that prisoners could put their name down and await their chance to play their beloved music. The 70s to us was the best decade for music and with prisoners having different tastes, we were treated to a wide repertoire of music and artists, many of which I had never heard of but began to admire. However, if the Sony Walkman had been invented by then, it certainly would have prevented many an argument over whose turn it was to play their record next.

Johnny Cash was setting the trend throughout the prisons in the USA with his famous concert at St Quentin. The internees requested that the prison allow some local artists in for a Christmas concert, but of course it was refused. We requested the same but it also was refused. We always stuck to the principle that if the prison didn't allow it then do it yourself, so we formed a concert committee to develop and deliver a Christmas pantomime. Of course we had all sorts of characters in the camp and plenty of wannabe singers and musicians. Joe Stitt was the 'Monty Python' of Long Kesh and quickly got a couple of his like friends together to organise entertainment for Christmas. Organising a concert in freedom was one thing, organising one in Long Kesh was much more challenging. The Concert Committee members were quite creative and talented. They set about drawing up a programme of song, scripts, comedy and acting. They went even further by making props from whatever they could get their hands on and smuggling in cloth and materials to make costumes and dresses. The sewing machines we used for handicrafts were hijacked for hours, as prisoners made every effort to make the pantomime as realistic as possible. Of course when it came to stockings, suspenders and other types of lingerie we had to smuggle them in and everyone who did so dreaded the thought of being caught. It would have been hard to explain. The Concert Committee even went to the extremes of erecting a makeshift stage and curtains. About two weeks before the concert was due on Christmas Eve, rehearsals began. Those participating in the Concert were excused drill, parades and general duties while they perfected their roles.

CHAPTER 21

Radio Free Long Kesh

COMMUNICATION WAS VITAL between the compounds and between the inside and the outside world. On the inside a simple tennis ball was used. It was slashed half way and messages could be put inside and then thrown over the wire into the next compound. Prior to the fire, the compounds in Phase 5 and Phase 6 were factional and sometimes we had to throw the balls into Republican compounds for them to throw into the next Loyalist compound or vice versa. This custom and practice was honoured by all. Then of course we could use the semaphore system, which was the quickest but had its drawbacks in darkness, especially in the winter.

Messages could also be passed during trips to the two football pitches in the centre of the phase (section). The pitches were surrounded by compounds of every faction, so when compound football teams were allowed out to play it gave them access to most of the compounds where they could chat with friends and also pass messages. The COs of each compound used the football matches as a means of getting together, drawing up policy and addressing problems. The prison regime knew this and they attempted to sabotage it by curtailing the numbers to 11 players each side, one referee and two linesmen. However, I quickly came up with the idea of Loyalists playing Gaelic football, thus allowing us 15 players each plus referee and linesmen. After the first match the prison regime gave up.

Visits were another opportunity to give verbal messages or smuggle out written messages to the outside, although we were limited in what we could say or write, and there was always the danger that the messages could be intercepted. The fire exposed the weaknesses in all of these. It left us with no means of communication to the outside and our worried families were left concerned for our safety and well being. It took about a year to get back to

123

where we where before the fire, when Phase 6 was rebuilt, only this time it housed all Loyalist compounds.

Joe Deane was a legendary 'radio ham' from the Highfield Estate who was thoroughly efficient in building radio transmitters and transmitting, In those early days of the conflict he was behind the various pirate radio stations that broadcast over Belfast in the 70s such as Radio Shankill, Radio Orange and Radio Free Ulster. Joe was a friend of Winston Rea who was now in Compound 21. Winston suggested smuggling in the parts of a radio transmitter and assembling it inside the prison. Joe provided us with a diagram and instructions on how to assemble the transmitter, which was smuggled into the camp by a visitor. Friends on the outside accumulated the parts and our imaginative 'Granny McCrea' smuggled them into the prison on her visits. The transmitter parts contained some of the largest valves of the time but 'Granny McCrea' managed it and within a few weeks we had all the necessary parts. It was now up to 'Alarm Clock Harry' our electrical genius to assemble the parts and produce the goods. Harry had the transmitter up and running in no time and now all we needed to do was to test the effectiveness of our new found toy.

Andy Spence had been consulting with Joe about the best way to set up the necessary aerial and conceal it from the prying eyes of passing army and police patrols. Andy ran 200 yards of aerial wire from his house in the Shankill Estate along the street, underneath the eaves of the roof, and was able to transmit and receive signals. The next stage was to develop a scheme that would enable us to make the transmitters compatible. I was asked to draw up some codes just like I had done with the semaphore system. We developed a scheme that when we wanted to talk we would continuously play the Eric Burdon and the Animals song, 'We Gotta Get Out of this Place' while our friends on the outside would play the Johnny Cash song 'I Walk the Line'. This worked quite well and enabled us to tune into each other's transmitters. So much time and effort had been put into this endeavour that the main priority was keeping it concealed during searches by the prison staff and the army. Someone came up with the idea of concealing it in the underbelly of the 'Burco' boilers that were used to boil water for tea in each of the huts. The bottom inside was taken apart and the radio was soldered into the bottom of the boiler. The casing was put back on, the boiler placed upright, filled with water and it became a tea boiler again.

This hiding place was never found and it proved an invaluable asset. Now no matter what was happening in the camp, we had the ability to send messages and information out to the big world outside. We also developed secret multiple codes so that we could transmit sensitive messages out undetected by the security forces. We didn't use it too often, keeping it for emergencies instead. It became invaluable during standoff situations or when prison officers took action and refused to provide visiting or mail services.

CHAPTER 22

Uisce Beatha

I SUPPOSE I should return to my Irish language lessons with Daciah Power, which included a bottle of Long Kesh poteen and instructions on how to make it. When I went back to C19 with instructions how to make the Long Kesh moonshine, Gusty insisted that it would be consumed only twice a year, at the 12 July and Christmas. We were all happy with that because the potency of the poteen was mindboggling. So I set about attempting to make my first batch. We smuggled in packets of brewing yeast and took 20 lbs of sugar, a pot of jam and a pot of treacle from our own stores. We approached our ingenious inventors and told them what we needed a still. The plastic bin was brought into the showers and scrubbed clean. Within a short time the inventors came back to me with a wonderful plan of how to make a collapsible still. They would remove two shower fittings from the shower room and connect them together. Using drainpipes, chair legs and leather hose, they would make a cooling system running through a fluorescent light cover into the toilet and connect it to the tea boiler that would be filled with 'the wash'. When we were finished with the still we could then dismantle it and put all the parts back in their rightful places. That way it would never be found during searches.

When dinner arrived all the prisoners donated their potatoes. The bin was set at the top of the hut and the potatoes were dumped into it. Hot water was poured in, and the sugar, treacle, jam and yeast followed, stirring the 'wash' all the time. The lid was then put on and a cap made from a sewn blanket fitted over the top. Now it was time to wait. There were two toilets at the top of the camp and we used one to store the bin away from the prying eyes of the prison officers. Each day I checked the 'wash' almost every hour when I should have just left it alone.

In prison we had a restricted timeline as the compound was searched every fortnight. We decided to let the 'wash' ferment for 11 days and on the twelfth day we would distil and bottle it, concealing the bottles and replacing the still parts to their respective places each day. So at 18 minutes before lock up time we removed two of eight showers from the ablutions and the drainpipe from the outside of the hut, and smuggled both inside. When the prison officers counted us and locked the doors it was go. The inventors constructed the still near the toilet and the bin was brought out to the centre of the floor. Everyone was asked to get their final cup of tea before we commandeered the tea boiler. The tea boiler was filled with 'wash' from the bin and then the rim and lid were sealed with bread and milk which hardened when heated and completely sealed the boiler. The boiler was turned on and we waited with patience for the alcohol to be vaporised in the boiler and then the still would be truly tested. We had about ten jars and one was put under the exiting shower pipe. It seemed like hours but eventually the clear liquid poteen began to trickle out of the pipe into the jar like a saline drip. We checked the quality of the poteen by dipping a piece of paper into the jar until the flame burned dry without burning the paper. It was good stuff so we sat up all night refilling the boiler until we had emptied the bin. We had filled nine jars and felt very proud of ourselves. We sealed the jars, concealed them in the roof of the hut, replaced the tea boiler, dismantled the still and cleaned the bin. When the doors opened the next morning and after the count, we smuggled out the shower fittings and replaced them in the ablutions along with the drainpipe. Two days later, prison officers entered the compound to search and we kept our fingers crossed that they wouldn't find our poteen. We were lucky this time but were uncomfortable with the hiding place, and not sure we could store the poteen there undiscovered until Christmas.

However, inspiration can come from the strangest places and it was provided by the prison camp itself. Every month a prison officer selected a film to show in the canteen of each compound. Our next film was the *French Connection*. We were sitting watching the film when a scene portrayed criminals opening tins, filling them, resealing the cans and smuggling them out of the country. Our poteen squad all looked at each other at the same time. After the film we got together to discuss how we could adopt this method to hide our poteen safely. It didn't take long to come up with an idea. One prisoner pierced a tin of Fanta and shook it so that the pressure of the gas poured the juice out of the can. He then held it over his cup until it all drained out and said that if we could get a syringe, we could syringe the poteen into the can and then solder the hole. We tested the theory and it worked. Immediately we retrieved all the jars from their hiding places and collected cans from prisoners, removing the contents and then injecting the cans of Coke and Fanta with poteen and soldering the holes. It was a brilliant idea and was never discovered during all the years I was there. Luckily, we had a soldering iron.

The semaphore system we established proved a vital means of communication during our whole time in Long Kesh. Here Ronnie McCullough, Fergus Robb, Harry Matthews and Stevie Clifford are receiving and sending messages.

Winston Rea and David Bates pose for a photograph in Compound 18. In the background beds sheets are strung over the barb wire in protest at the failure of the prison authorities to honour their pledge of a weekly change of bed linen.

An aerial view of Long Kesh after the compounds were burnt by Republican prisoners in October 1974. As you can see, Compound 19, as the single Loyalist compound in Phase 6 at the time, is the only one still standing. *(Open Government Licence 2.0)*

A photograph of me with the wire clippers we used to get out of the compounds during the burning of the camp by Republicans.

An image of two soldiers manhandling a Republican prisoner during a riot on one of the occasions when the Army was called into Long Kesh. In the background, other prisoners are lined up against a wall to be searched. *(Imperial War Museum, HU 70205)*

British soldiers in riot gear confront Republican prisoners through a compound fence during a riot in Long Kesh. The ground is littered with stones and other missiles hurled at the troops by the rioters. *(Imperial War Museum, HU 70209)*

The fight for proper education took a whole new meaning when the Open University came to the prison. Here is William Strain, the first Loyalist to gain a degree through the Open University in Long Kesh.

The Open University went from strength to strength with several more Loyalists gaining a degree.

The inside cover of a prison book where I had written down phrases in Irish during my lessons.

Handicrafts made by
prisoners in Long Kesh
from leather, wood and
matchsticks.

More handicrafts and an old Singer treadle-powered sewing machine.

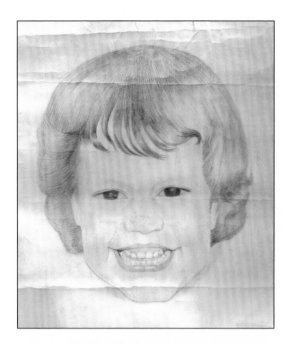

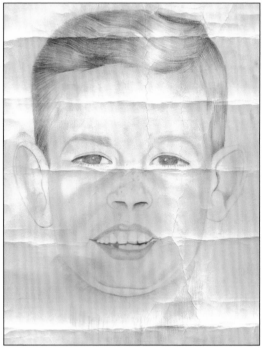

William McConnell was great at sketching with just a pencil and spent a lot of time sketching prisoner's children from photographs.

Freddie Stevenson was our first artist and brightened up the huts with his murals. This one was titled 'Thrashing oats with flails'.

Sketches of prison guards made by George Morrow.

George Morrow, December 1976

George Morrow, 'Morning Frost', December 1976

George Morrow, 'Compound 19', January 1977

George was probably one of the most talented artists in Long Kesh. He spent most of his time painting and sketching real time moments, making his collection a pictorial history of Long Kesh.

George Morrow, February 1977

A display showing a replica of the poteen still and hidden radio we used within Long Kesh.

UVF/RHC prisoners with real weapons inside Long Kesh, made from lengths of a basketball stanchion, which was equivalent to a 12 bore shotgun.

Myself (left) with Jim Glendinning and Ronnie McCullough a few weeks after their release.

Making a speech after joining the Transport and General Workers Union.

Compound 19 in Long Kesh in more recent times.

The entrance gates to Compound 19. *(Copyright GiollaUidir, Creative Commons ShareAlike 2.5 Generic Licence.)*

The typical Nissen huts within the compounds.

Inside the huts. After the fire we negotiated this partitioned style of accommodation for more privacy.

I returned to Compound 19 to make a DVD for Community Television.

Former UVF leader and Loyalist icon Gusty Spence (right) announces the Loyalist ceasefire in 1994 along with (left to right) David Adams, David Ervine, Gary McMichael and myself. (*Pacemaker Press*)

CHAPTER 23

Ending of Special Category Status

WHEN THE TROUBLES erupted in 1969 in Belfast and violence spread throughout Northern Ireland, the obvious result, beside the death and destruction, was that more people were entering the prison system. However, the prisoners who were now flooding the old Victorian Belfast Prison were of a different type. They were prisoners of the conflict and did not believe they were 'criminals'. They did not subscribe nor succumb to the inhuman, degrading and penitence psyche prevalent throughout all prisons in the United Kingdom.

Gusty Spence had been in Crumlin Road Prison's A Wing from 1966 along with about 20 other Loyalists, with other Loyalists spread throughout the remaining B, C and D Wings. The Official IRA was the dominant force, but the PIRA prisoners soon became prominent as the violence continued to spew more prisoners into the prison. Gusty Spence represented all Loyalists at that time and Bruce McMenemy was second in command. Francis Card and Billy McKee were in charge of PIRA prisoners and Peter Monaghan was in charge of Official IRA prisoners.

The regime, conditions, treatment and overcrowding at Crumlin Road Prison were a catalyst for all factions to work separately yet toward the same goal, fighting for political status. Loyalists could not be seen to be working closely together with Republicans as they would not get any support for such actions from their own community, so they devised a strategy to circumvent that perception. PIRA prisoners had decided to go on hunger strike with Francis Card and Billy McKee leading the charge. Loyalists agreed to engage in acts of sabotage and protests to put more pressure on the Government. The UDA, Loyalist women and other Loyalist groupings agreed to hold nightly protests outside the prison in support of the fight for political status. In July 1972, the prison Governor met all the representatives of the different factions and explained to them that there was an offer on the table from the Governor.

Prisoners sentenced for conflict related offences would be given a new title known as 'Special Category Prisoners':

• They would be granted one visit per week.

• They would be allowed to wear their own clothes.

• They would be able to refrain from prison work.

• There would be a review of prison conditions and facilities.

• They had been granted political status in everything but name.

Upon acceptance they were taken in groups down to the prison reception where they were given their personal possessions and civilian clothes, and then returned to their cells.

Later that night William Whitelaw announced the introduction of Special Category Status in Parliament. I spoke to one prisoner who told me the change from criminal to 'Special Category Prisoner' was so quick and smooth that day shift prison staff were not even informed. When a prison officer opened his cell the next morning and he appeared in his civilian clothing, the officer immediately threw him back into his cell and locked him up. He refused to let him out until a senior prison officer came and explained to him what had occurred during the night.

On the 4 November 1975 the then Secretary of State Merlyn Rees announced that as from the 1 March 1976 the Government would begin phasing out Special Category Status. Anyone convicted of a scheduled offence after that date would not be granted the Status introduced by Willie Whitelaw in 1972. We knew that something was brewing for a long time because we could see a new style prison being built from the roofs of our huts in Long Kesh. These curious constructions were a compound system like Long Kesh but instead of Nissen huts they were using bricks to build a strange cell block that later took its name from its shape, 'H' Blocks. At first we thought they were going to try to force us into them but I think they knew we were too disciplined and organised so they decided not to.

The decision to end Special Category Status certainly put the prison system in a whole new light and would plunge the whole prison population into another dangerous phase of conflict. There was also an accompanying decision to introduce 50 per cent remission of prison sentences. New prisoners didn't go to the camp but instead went directly to the 'H' Blocks. We remained in the compounds until gradually the numbers went down. Negotiations took place in 1986 and the few remaining Special Category Prisoners then went to the 'H' Blocks but kept their Special Category Status.

We had been negotiating with the NIO for half remission of sentences and other concessions that can be seen in a letter from Long Kesh to prisoners in Magilligan.

Compound 18
Long Kesh Camp

To the OCs UVF/RHC Prisoners
Magilligan Camp

November 1975

In view of the recent controversy relating to Merlyn Rees's speech in the House of Commons pertaining to prisoners in Northern Ireland I feel it incumbent to spell out, as far as I am prepared at this time, the Official UVF/RHC reaction and policies.

With regard to the proposed 'half sentence' release scheme, I have had talks with the NIO to have certain misgivings clarified, and am now satisfied with the proposed scheme, therefore, the official stand the UVF/RHC shall take on this issue is to accept it. This scheme permits men who have served half of their sentences to be released just as the present system allows releases after serving two-thirds of their sentence.

I am fully aware that 'lifers' cannot see any positive benefit from this scheme, but I can assure that whatever can be done is being done in order to have men serving 'life' sentences released at the earliest date possible. However, much could depend on the prevailing situation in freedom. Furthermore, it would be unwise for Merlyn Rees to publicly announce to the effect that men serving 'life' sentences would be given concessions.

The aspect of Rees's proposals which relate to the termination of incoming Special Category Prisoners from March 1st 1976 will be dealt with at a more practical date. It would be precipitous to make conclusive policies about this aspect at the time. This issue will be dealt with separately from the others.

I have already recently partaken in negotiations with the NIO concerning the issue of compassionate parole. Our views were documented and presented to the NIO official and I have forwarded you with a copy of this document. The position is:

1) I have not as yet made any commitment to allow or prevent any UVF/RHC Prisoner from accepting Christmas parole as is possible. Christmas parole will not be affected by the negotiations about compassionate parole.

2) I am satisfied that my negotiations re. Compassionate parole will prove successful and I will inform you accordingly of the outcome.

3) It must be stressed that any UVF/RHC prisoner who may be granted parole of whatever description must abide by the declared UVF/RHC policies and be of good behaviour for the duration of his parole. Furthermore, all UVF/RHC parolees will return to the place of imprisonment on the time and date specified by the authorities.

Whenever any UVF/RHC prisoner goes on parole the word of his organisation is at stake therefore, the onus is on all parolees to ensure that our word remains our bond. Any UVF/RHC parolee who causes a breach of these of these instructions shall be severely disciplined.

This is practically all I have to state at this time, but you can be assured that I will keep you up to date with regard to my decisions and with any issues which may concern you.

Signed _____

AA Spence Commanding Officer

Continuing negotiations eventually reduced the tariff that life sentence prisoners would have to serve before they appeared before the Parole Board and compassionate parole rules were also relaxed.

As 1 March loomed, tensions within all the prisons rose, but although the cut off date was finite, by the time remand prisoners were processed through the judicial system it would not be until September that the first prisoners began to enter the 'H' Blocks at the Maze. Despite popular belief, Loyalists at first refused to wear prison clothes but after a few weeks we could not get any support for such action from the Unionist community as it was seen as joining with the IRA. The situation inside the prisons turned sour and Crumlin Road Prison and the 'H' Blocks became the focal points.

CHAPTER 24

Imprisoned UVF/RHC Prisoners

ON THE 2 November 1976 the UVF/RHC Camp Council sent out the following statement with regard to the ending of Special Category Status and consequent disturbances in Crumlin Road Prison:

> The Camp Council consisting of the Commanding Officer, Compounds 18, 19, and 21 OCs and Adjutant of the UVF/RHC personnel do pledge that we shall support our comrades throughout the UVF/RHC in freedom, in their struggle to resist the removal of 'Special Category Status' from our colleagues who are charged with offences committed after the 1st March this year.
>
> Furthermore, we give the present leadership of the UVF/RHC our complete support in the task they have before them, and we are prepared to engage in extreme action within this Camp in order to give actual support to the fight for an acceptable settlement of the 'political status' issue. We are renowned for our responsible demeanour within Long Kesh, but we are equally renowned for our discipline and determination if we believe that principles require specific action from us. In this instance we believe it may be necessary to embark upon drastic action in order to extract an acceptable formula, therefore we state that if it is warranted and necessary the UVF/RHC contingent in Long Kesh will not be found wanting. We wish you all every success in the campaign for 'political status'.
>
> Signed AA Spence (Commanding Officer)
>
> James Strutt OC C18, R Warnock OC C19, R McCullough OC C21
>
> Trevor King Adjutant

In response to this statement a communiqué was received from the outside to Long Kesh after prisoners had sent out queries about communication and progress regarding the opposition to the ending of Special Category Status:

From Brigade to AA Spence 26/11/76

1) Disciplinary Action

At the present time steps are being taken to draw up a code of conduct, which shall be implemented throughout the organisations. Anyone who fails to abide by this shall be dealt with, irrespective of who they are, or what they are. We fully realise that there have been discrepancies in the past but we shall endeavour to eradicate this in the future.

In order to help us achieve this, it would be appreciated if any information which is obtained during the debriefing, which takes place in the prisons, was made available to the "committee" which has been set up on the outside. We are aware that this has been done on occasions in the past but no action has been taken on the information received, but can assure you that this will not now be the case from now on.

2) Political Status

Re: negotiations on political status. It was suggested to you by Jim McDonald that you in fact endeavour to open talks with the NIO with a view to arriving at an acceptable compromise to all parties. Since then a Joint Committee has been set up with the UDA with a view to pursuing all avenues open to us to achieve this. The UVF/RHC reps are Jim McDonald, Hugh Smith and two others. The UDA reps are Jim Craig, Eddie Martin, Billy Wilson and Harry Chicken.

We are in full agreement that any policy or action decided upon will be presented as a united front and we would expect that at any meetings which would take place either 'inside or outside' at least two preferably three of the above panel would be in attendance.

This would ensure that all personnel both 'inside and outside' would be fully aware that any interested Republican groups would be included in these negotiations and have no objections to this.

In closing, on this particular question we would like to emphasise the solidarity that exists on the outside between the UVF/RHC/UDA and would like to think the same could be said of the inside.

3) Sectarian Assassinations
Before the UVF/RHC would contemplate taking part in any talks, there would have to be a cessation of violence. This would include the murders of UDR, RUC and Army personnel and also the Republican's term of economic bombings. In fact it would have to be just exactly what is stated above. A COMPLETE CESSATION OF VIOLENCE.

4) H Block
In order to clear any misunderstanding that may exist concerning H Block. H Block is part and parcel of Long Kesh, all UVF/RHC in H Block come under the command of Long Kesh Commanding Officer ie AA Spence. We realise that there may be problems re communication with H Block but are confident the CO will be able to overcome it.

5) Long Kesh Documents
We are aware that in the past a lot of documents received from Long Kesh have been 'mislaid' or cast aside but would assure you that this will not happen again. In future any correspondence received from any camp will be discussed by Brigade Staff and Battalion Commanders and an explicit reply shall be sent back.

We shall also endeavour at all times to keep all personnel informed as to the policy of the UVF/RHC and shall adopt whatever policy is thought to be in the best interests of the Loyalist people of Ulster.

These decisions would eventually lead to the end of the prison system and control that we had campaigned for from the very moment we entered Long Kesh. The conditions we had fought for and the educational achievements we had attained in that sparse, bleak and unfriendly steel desert I had entered in 1972 would now be a thing of the past. The fact that no more prisoners would join us after 1 March 1976 coupled with the 50 per cent remission meant that our numbers in the camp would be drastically reduced within the coming year. The concrete construction site we could see from our huts was rapidly overshadowing the camp, but little did we know what horrors these 'H' blocks would bring in the future.

CHAPTER 25

Escapes (Part 2)

AFTER ALL SENTENCED prisoners were moved back to Long Kesh in December 1972, escape attempts were numerous but unsuccessful. The closest we came to success was with Stevie McCrea, a member of the RHC who was serving life for the assassination of a Catholic. In 1976, the prison authorities announced that they were bringing a mobile X-ray machine into the camp to X-ray every prisoner to check their health. We suspected it was more to do with the outcry about the CR Gas that was used during the fire of October 1974 but we reluctantly agreed to take part in this so-called health initiative. The X-ray machine entered the camp on the Monday. It was just like a caravan and was towed into the middle of Phase 5 to begin its medical experiment on the prisoners in C9, C10, C11, C12, C13 and C14. When we were passing the caravan while going to visits, Stevie McCrea said to us: "Well if it comes into the camp it has to go out of the camp." Already his mind was working overtime as he tried to draw up a plan using the X-ray machine to help him escape from the camp.

The X-ray machine finally ended up in Phase 6 consisting of C16, C17, C18, C19, C20 and C21. We were the last prisoners to undergo these tests and Stevie McCrea approached the camp escape committee for approval of his audacious but simple plan. He believed he could get to the mobile caravan, hide underneath it during the day and then sneak into it that night. As we were the last prisoners to be X-rayed, Stevie hoped the mobile would leave the camp with him inside it. The escape plan was approved and everyone concerned was told of the part they would play. The two main hurdles were to get Stevie out of the compound, under the noses of the prison officers to the X-ray van and then to cover his absence while the X-ray van was in the camp. We estimated we would only have to cover his absence for 24 hours. We were in C21 and all day we watched as the rows upon rows of prisoners exited from each compound and lined up at the mobile van to be X-rayed. There were about 350 prisoners in Phase 6, and the prison authorities were in a rush to have them all done in one day. We observed the way the prison officers were supervising the prisoners. Whether through laziness, boredom or lack of manpower, they were letting prisoners in and out of their compounds to go to for X-ray without counting them in or out. This was a massive lapse in security and we prisoners noticed it readily. This would make things a lot easier.

Halfway through the volume of C21, prisoners Stevie McCrea and Ronnie McCullough walked out the compound gates towards the mobile van and got their X-rays. The prison officer on duty at the gate of C21 was a Welsh man who we obviously called 'Taffy'. Taffy would talk the leg off a stool and was always good for a chat. Ronnie McCullough, who was camp second in command, pretended to usher more prisoners towards the van and Taffy was very grateful for this and thanked him profusely. Meanwhile Stevie McCrea slipped out behind him. Taffy shook Ronnie's hand while Stevie rolled under the van and it was as simple as that. A prisoner who was on an afternoon visit smuggled a letter out, to be taken to a colleague on the outside informing him of the situation. Upon receipt of the letter, two armed active service units numbering eight men were immediately called upon to rescue Stevie from the van as it left Long Kesh. Two cars were hijacked and the owners warned not to report it for 24 hours. The units and cars were taken to a safe farm nearby to Long Kesh and covered up. The front gates of the camp were put under surveillance to watch for the X-ray van leaving the prison.

It would be a long night for Stevie as he lay under the van and darkness fell on the camp. We had our role to play as we had to cover for one missing person. The protocol for locking up and the head count was pretty relaxed. One prison officer entered the hut and everybody lined up both sides of the hut and faced each other. As the prison officer walked up the hut one prisoner who had been pre-nominated did the 'Long Kesh shuffle' across the floor after being counted so that he would be counted again. We all held our breath as one mistake would reveal the escape attempt, but the prisoner was so quiet and so quick that we didn't even see him move ourselves. The prison officer came up to him for the second time, counted him and then walked on, said goodnight and locked the doors. We breathed a sigh of relief and we were excited at things having gone so well thus far.

In the middle of the night Stevie sneaked into the X-ray van and hid in a cupboard, pulled covers over him and settled down for the night. We believed that the X-ray van would leave the prison the next day and the active service units would intercept it on the outside and rescue Stevie. We made a false skeletal dummy with false hair and a papier mache head. In the morning some of us were up when the prison officers entered the hut. We made tea and some of us had our washing kit ready to go to the ablutions as normal, and the prison officer just strolled through the hut unaware that one of the bodies was nothing more than a dummy. It worked, so we knew that there were no more counts until 9.00 pm that evening. At about 12 noon the X-ray machine was moved out of Phase 6 towards the front of the camp and the front gate, so we kept our fingers crossed that soon Stevie McCrea would once again be in freedom.

For hours we were uptight not knowing whether it had been successful or not. Then a prisoner coming back from parole through the reception area reported to us that he had seen the X-ray machine sitting parked beside the internee compounds near the front of the camp. This was a setback, as thought that the machine would be taken out that morning. The active service units on the outside would also be nervous that the X-ray machine hadn't appeared. Immediately the semaphorists sent messages down to C9, the nearest compound to the X-ray machine, to give us a signal when it moved. The semaphorists remained at their post until dark and the van was still there. On an afternoon visit a further message was sent out to the active service Commander relaying the position of the van in the camp. This heightened tensions both inside and outside the camp, as armed men in hijacked cars were sitting waiting for hours and could be uncovered at any time. Inside it meant that we had to do the 'Long Kesh shuffle' again and we were unsure whether we would be able to get away with it two nights in a row. About five minutes before lockup we were in our huts getting ready to go through the ruse one more time. The same prisoner was nominated to do the 'shuffle' again but we were less confident this second night, as a different prison officer was on duty and we weren't sure what demeanour he would adopt when counting. Most officers were in a hurry to finish their shift and get to their in-house bar in 'silver city', so we tried the 'shuffle' again. It was performed as sweetly as the night before and worked so we could relax until the next morning.

As the doors opened in the morning, the same 'dummy' was counted as a live prisoner, so we just prayed that the X-ray machine would leave that day. By dinner time the machine was still in the camp and we were still using messages smuggled out in visits to keep outside informed, as we thought they were in more danger than us. However, the active service units were well hidden in safe houses in the surrounding area. The tension and strain on everyone concerned intensified as the day passed by and there was no movement around the X-ray van. So, for a third night, we did the 'shuffle' and managed to get away with it yet again. The dummy did its job the next morning also but we knew that sooner or later the prison officers would catch on.

Stevie told us later that during the three nights he would sneak out in the early hours of the morning to lie underneath the van for a stretch and also to relieve himself. The fourth day arrived and we knew that neither inside nor outside could maintain the operation for much longer. At about 12 noon the X-ray machine was hooked up to a civilian jeep and began to move towards the front gates. The semaphorists exchanged messages and we were excited as now was the final testing point of our plan. The X-ray machine passed all the inner gates until it came to a halt at the final checkpoint. Stevie told us later that the sergeant in charge had searched the van and he had evaded detection but that a new guard shift had just arrived and insisted on searching the van again. On the second search, the escape attempt was foiled and all hell broke loose as they tried to ascertain who the prisoner was that they had captured. Stevie was a life sentence prisoner, so it was useless charging him. Instead he ended up getting 56 days of solitary confinement and the nickname Stevie 'X-Ray' McCrea.

Of course there were other individual escapologists who created opportunities. One such man was Tommy McAllister from the South Belfast area, who was serving eight years for explosive related charges. He ate gravel from the football pitch and made himself sick. He was taken to the prison hospital where they suspected he had possible gall stone problems and recommended he be sent to the Royal Victoria Hospital in Belfast for examination. Tommy was taken to the hospital under armed guard where he was examined and X-rayed. Doctors were unsure of the findings so they decided to keep Tommy overnight for observation.

The private side ward was four floors up so the prison guards thought it secure enough and kept guard outside the door. Tommy had other ideas.

He wedged the window open inch by inch in the early hours of the morning while the prison guards were half sleeping outside the door of the ward. He noticed a drainpipe a few feet away so slid out of the window and manoeuvred over to it. Quick as a flash he shimmied down the pipe and was gone. He remained in freedom for two years before he was arrested in a caravan park in the County Down resort of Millisle. Needless to say he was not allowed near football pitches anymore.

Though Loyalists tried many times to tunnel out of the Kesh, we never seemed to capture the art of tunnelling. It was either too short, too shallow or we would be discovered before we reached our goal. On our first attempt at a tunnel, the shaft was not deep enough and when two prison officers were patrolling around the compound it collapsed and one of the officers fell into it!

CHAPTER 26

Guns Behind the Wire

By the summer of 1976 the camp had been rebuilt from the ashes of the fire, only this time we were divided along factional lines. Phase 6 was comprised of C16, C17 and C20 (housing UDA prisoners), and C18, C19 and C21 (housing UVF/RHC Prisoners). The former perimeter wall now separated us from all Republican prisoners, similar to the Berlin Wall. This situation meant that there was less interaction between Republicans and Loyalists, and the Camp Council became that much more difficult to continue with its progressive political ideology. The UVF/RHC formed their three compounds into their own Camp Council, so that each compound acted as one and no one was left abandoned.

The internecine conflict between Loyalist factions on the outside was never far away. However, we as prisoners expected that everyone coming into the camp, from whatever faction, would leave those problems and their negative attitudes on the outside, just like we did between Loyalists and Republicans under the 'No Conflict Policy'. Relationships were normal, they were in their compounds and we were in ours, they ran their compounds, we ran ours, and there was no outward animosity toward each other. We were unaware however, that a power struggle was taking place within the UDA compounds and structures were being undermined. There were now a number of prisoners in the camp who had been involved in feuding between the organisations and had brought the hatred for each other into the camp. A new UDA Commander had been appointed, as Jimmy Craig, the long term commander had just been released. The new commander was finding it difficult to control this element, but it was an issue for the UDA organisation outside to resolve.

Other than that we did not at that time feel under threat from anyone and were content under the policy of 'no conflict'. Two members of the UVF within Compound 21 were convicted of offences connected with feuds, but there were prisoners of that ilk within all factions. One day, one of these prisoners, Norman Cooke, went on a visit as normal, taking the prison van to the visiting area. He had requested an extended visit with his wife for welfare reasons, so was granted a one hour visit instead of half an hour. Trevor King and Bobby Spence from C21, who were not in prison for feud related offences, were also on a visit that day but returned in the prison van after the usual half hour. I and two other prisoners were walking around our compound when we noticed some unusual behaviour around the gates of C17 and C20. The prison van containing Bobby Spence and Trevor King was suddenly being pursued by two groups of UDA prisoners, who had just scaled the wire fences. The leading two UDA prisoners, who we could see were in possession of two hand guns, were closing in on the van, with the mob behind them. Immediately we gave the alarm and every UVF/RHC prisoner emerged from the huts and formed up in ranks, ready to scale the wire fences. The quick thinking of the prison officer driving the van saved their lives. He drove on past C21 towards the large gates leading to the football fields. The officer on duty quickly opened the gates, allowed the van through and closed them again, preventing the assailants from pursuing the van any further. It was obvious to us that not all UDA prisoners were party to this attack, as C16 and most of the prisoners in C17 and C20 remained in their compounds.

Billy Sloan, the new UDA Commander in the camp, emerged from C16 and ordered all UDA prisoners back to their respective compounds. He immediately sought out Gusty Spence and reassured him that it was not an authorised attack and he would deal with those who had lead it. It was a sad day and I felt sick because we had friends in all the compounds and now the 'no conflict policy' that had survived so many tests, including the fire, had been broken by fellow Loyalists. Although tensions remained high, they were now controllable. Over the next few days many UDA prisoners in conversations with us criticised those who led the attack. Trevor King and Bobby Spence were able to return to our compound unharmed.

The breach of trust was a thing we could not ignore, however, and we implored Gusty to allow us to smuggle guns into the camp. He was resistant to having weapons in the camp and had refused the same request after the fire on the basis that the 'no conflict policy' had not been infringed. This time however it had been broken and he reluctantly agreed. We immediately set about looking at ways and means of getting weapons into the camp for our own defence in exceptional circumstances. We estimated it would take a few weeks. It always amazed me that whenever we were in a tight position in Long Kesh there was always a prisoner who popped up with the most amazing plan or solution. The 'mechanic' came to us and stated that he could make us guns in a matter of minutes – all we needed was to do was to smuggle in the ammunition. We knew the 'mechanic' could do almost anything with his skilful hands but we still looked at him as if he was a nutcase. He brought three of us out to the compound yard where there were basketball stanchions and said, "Here lads, there's your guns." We looked at each other, then at him and asked him to explain. He pointed to the stanchions and told us they were the same diameter as a 12 gauge shot gun. All we had to do was cut them into barrel lengths and using a bed end which fitted neatly over the barrel end, affix a firing pin and we had a makeshift shot gun. Apparently the 'mechanic' used to shuffle round the compound and huts looking for ideas and making all sorts of gadgets for all sorts of enterprises. He had stumbled upon this invention some time before so when we needed guns he was confident he had the solution.

The next day we damaged the stanchions, making it look like an accident so it wouldn't arouse suspicion with the prison staff. We cut four barrel lengths with a hacksaw and then inserted a firing mechanism in a bed end and it fitted over the barrels like a glove. All we needed now were the cartridges. Without doubt our greatest smuggler into Long Kesh was Granny McCrea, the granny of Stevie McCrea. She visited Stevie every week and the things she smuggled in were unbelievable. We had the cartridges delivered to her and within three weeks she had smuggled in eight cartridges. We removed the gunpowder from one cartridge, tested the weapons and everything seemed to be in order. Now the crucial thing was to find a hide where they would not be uncovered during a search. We removed the cross beams on the front doors, channelled them out the same diameter as the barrels, fitted them back on, and they were perfect. We never had to use them and they were never uncovered – I believe they are still there.

The UDA Inner Council on the outside responded quickly to the actions of the renegade UDA prisoners by sending the following communiqué into the prison:

From: The Supreme Commander
Ulster Defence Association
Headquarters Belfast

To: Compound 16
Long Kesh Prison Camp

Thursday 28 July 1976

To be read out to all UDA Personnel: Long Kesh

As from this date Mr William Sloan has been appointed by me as commanding officer and John White will be his second in command. A command structure will be set up within the camp by the two aforementioned men and no one will presume to usurp their authority. The commanding officers' appointment has been made by me personally and Mr Sloan will be answerable to me and no other person. Officers and NCOs will be designated by Mr Sloan without fear or favour and it will not matter what part of Ulster an officer or NCO hails from. Mr Sloan and his officers will be solely responsible for discipline, control and will at all times uphold the good name of the UDA.

Any officer or volunteer who fails to obey without hesitation or questions any orders directed to him by Mr Sloan and his Staff renders himself liable to court martial, which could result in relinquishment of political status and subsequent removal to Crumlin Road Prison.

It is my earnest desire that all my volunteers give their full allegiance to Mr Sloan and his command staff in the onerous and heavy responsibilities that await them.

All orders from the outside will be transmitted through Mr Sloan or responsible persons designated by him. Orders emanating from sources other than me personally will be disregarded. This document will be read out to all assembled UDA personnel without comment or opinions expressed.

In Comradeship
Signed _____
Supreme Commander, Ulster Defence Association

The new appointed UDA Commander and his officers then sought a meeting with the UVF command structure and the following agreement was drawn up and signed by the commanding officers of the UVF/RHC and the UDA.

> This document is to testify that a non-aggression pact exists between all UDA and UVF/RHC personnel contained in Long Kesh.
>
> It means that no planned or spontaneous attacks will take place by one faction upon another.
>
> It will be fully understood that if such circumstances do arise to cause agitation or apprehension between the two groupings, dialogue will take place with the sole purpose of ensuring that the 'no conflict' policy would remain inviolate.
>
> If certain individuals from time to time fail to obey the instructions of their faction officers and break the 'no conflict' agreement it is agreed that the faction to which the 'offender' belongs discipline him and the punishment be commensurate with offence. The punishment will be made to the aggrieved faction; personalities are of no consequence. It is our intent, taking into consideration the volatile nature of our environment, to renew this agreement yearly starting one year from today.
>
> In conclusion, and to manifest our sincerity we hereby affix our names below in the belief that peace and harmony not only can, but must exist between Loyalist factions. We must be servants of the Loyalist people and do only those things they would want us to do.
>
> Signed: _____
> Gusty Spence (UVF/RHC)
> William Sloan (UDA)

A short time later this pact was to be tested in full. In C21 Ronnie McCullough and Hugh Craig from Comber were walking round the compound when Hugh recognised a prison officer who was also from Comber. He began chatting to him and when he thought the opportunity arose he asked him would he smuggle a camera into the prison. The prison officer seemed to go along with the approach and said he would get it in a few days, so Hugh and Ronnie continued their walk around the compound. About an hour later the assistant Governor and two chief officers arrived at the Officers Hut just at the gates of the compound. A prison officer entered the compound and informed Gusty that the Governor had requested to see him.

Gusty thought it was something trivial until the Governor stated that one of his prison officers had been approached and threatened by two prisoners, Ronnie McCullough and Hugh Craig, to smuggle an illegal item, namely a camera, into the prison. Gusty asked if there was any corroborating evidence or just the word of one prison officer against two prisoners. This was always a thorn in prisoners' sides, where on the word of any prisoner officer, a prisoner could be found guilty of whatever he was accused of. The Governor insisted that he wanted the two prisoners handed over to be taken to the punishment cells but Gusty informed him that we would not be handing anyone over without proper procedure. At that point Gusty returned to the compound and gathered us all together in the canteen hut. He made us aware of the situation and warned us of the consequences if we didn't hand over our two comrades. We felt strongly about this issue because anyone of us could be falsely accused and punished without proper redress. Every prisoner to a man supported the decision not to hand our comrades over.

Our well rehearsed battle plans swung into action again and we began to prepare for a confrontation with the newly-formed prison officer riot squad. Semaphorists took to the roofs and began signalling to the UVF/RHC compounds, C18 and C19. The UDA compounds, C20, C16 and C17, were also informed. The new treaty between the UVF/RHC and UDA would now be tested and we were unsure whether it would be adhered to. In C21 gym equipment was jammed against the compound gates and men were deployed with wire cutters incase we became trapped in the compound. We all knew the drill well and within 15 minutes we were all at our posts, anxious but ready. We all watched the semaphorists closely for any movements to suggest the riot squad was on their way. The squad's most likely way in was through a large gate that led to the football fields and sure enough the UDA prisoners in C16 were soon signalling that the squad were gathering on the pitches. C16 updated us on the riot squad's every movement, as the prison officers who weren't part of the riot squad withdrew from the area. In those situations no one knows how things will develop or who is going to be seriously injured.

The large gate leading from the football fields opened and 150 black riot clad prison officers emerged in their ranks and marched towards C21. The majority of prisoners in C16, C17, C18, C19 and C20 remained in their huts waiting orders. The riot squad approached the gates of C21 and a senior prison officer called out for us to hand over Ronnie McCullough and Hugh

Craig. They were told politely that this would not happen and the standoff began. About five minutes later we could hear orders being given by the riot squad leaders, so we signalled to the other compounds. We didn't know exactly how many of the compounds would support us besides C18 and C19 but we didn't have to wait long for an answer. Prisoners rushed out of their huts, commandeered the gates of C18 and C19, and flooded onto the road. UDA prisoners in C16, C17 and C20 simultaneously commandeered their compounds and also flooded onto the road. Each compound brought a hand wheeled food truck with them and marched toward the lines of the riot squad. Things were now reversed, as the riot squad were surrounded and outnumbered by over 450 Loyalist prisoners. I don't know who planned the squad's tactics or what possessed them to think the other compounds wouldn't come to our aid, but they were now in deep shit.

The prisoners from the five other compounds were drawing closer to the squad and upon the orders of prison leaders, groups wheeling the trucks ran them at speed into the ranks of the riot squad. The squad was in disarray and began to retreat back towards the gate of the football fields. Under orders, the prisoners didn't pursue them but instead reinforced defences outside of C21. Signallers in C16 informed us that British Army riot troops were now pouring into the football fields as reinforcements. It was the first time since the fire of 1974 that the British Army had been deployed as riot troops inside the camp but we were prepared. Some of our prisoners had moulded parts of plastic chairs into protective pads for their arms and legs, and were assigned to fend off any war dogs. The Army formed up in ranks behind the prison officers but no one made a move to attack. Since the fire, there was an obvious political reluctance to use British troops in the front line – they were deployed more to support the prison officers who hadn't much stomach for a fight. The assistant Governor who started the whole thing then appeared with two chief prison officers. Both Gusty, the UVF/RHC Commander and Billy Sloan, the UDA Commander approached the three to begin negotiations, however, there was not much give or take. We demanded:

1) That the two prisoners would remain in the compound that night and appear before a Governor in the morning, and have representation from an officer.

2) All the prisoners would return to their respective compounds and a head count would be allowed.

3) There would be no retribution by staff or army or any other kind of mistreatment of any prisoner.

Points 2 and 3 were accepted but they wouldn't give in to point 1. The negotiators returned to their respective places without agreement. On hearing about the stalemate, the two prisoners concerned approached the senior officers of all the organisations and offered to hand themselves over, providing it was guaranteed that they would not be mistreated while in the punishment block. They felt that the point had been made and were content enough to end the deadlock. The negotiations resumed and the Prison authorities accepted the terms.

A friendly prison officer later told us that he overheard the riot squad taking in the prison officer's Mess and one of them said, "thank God it was sorted out because half of them characters are in for murder and they wouldn't think twice of killing one of us". Needless to say the riot squad was never sent into Phase 6 again.

CHAPTER 27

Collective Punishment

THE DIRTY PROTEST and fight for political status ensured that prison officers rose up the PIRA target table. More prison officers were assassinated during this period than at any other time in prison history. On 8 October 1976, RJ Hamilton became the third serving prison officer to be shot dead in this latest campaign by the Provisional IRA. He was stationed in Magilligan Camp and was shot dead outside his home in Londonderry. Prison officers under control of the Prison Officers Association (POA) immediately took retaliatory action and stopped all prison visits, parcels, newspapers, mail etc in every prison in Northern Ireland. The problem for us was that prison officers always took action that affected every prisoner in the camp, so we were being punished for something that was completely out of our control. This forced Gusty Spence, as CO, to pen two letters of protest, one to the Prison Officers Association and two to the UVF Brigade Staff.

Long Kesh Prison Camp

Ulster Volunteer Force
Belfast Headquarters

Saturday 9th October 1976

Before charges and counter charges are bandied about I want to set on record the true and relevant facts concerning the prison officers' action after one of their associates had been murdered in Derry. I agree that the staff of prisons should be interested solely in welfare and rehabilitation as quoted by the leader of the Prison Officers Association and must not be seen acting the role of a paramilitary group. I disagree that they act impartially simply because they stopped visits by prisoners' relatives whilst at the same time facilitated visits by clergy and solicitors. What prisoner wants to see a solicitor instead of his wife or children? Therefore the prison officers have discriminated to the detriment of the prisoners' loved ones whilst at the same time keeping a close eye on their public image. It would not do to get the clergy or the legal profession upset compared to some 'wee woman' from the back streets who happens to be a prisoner's wife. Nobody will pay any attention to her!

I will not beat about the bush nor shall I be hypocritical about the situation. I understand the prison officers feelings but what they are doing is hurting innocent people, women and children and they cannot justify that. If they are saying they are holding our families as hostage to ensure that no prison officers are hurt or killed then let them come out into the open and say that.

Their present action is outside prison rules and regulations and if we, as prisoners, were to go outside the law in here we would be punished for our 'crime'. The prison officers are also in breach of contract which they agreed when they joined the service.

The UVF/RHC have not been engaged in any attacks on prison officers or their families or homes nor, do I suppose, do we ever intend to do so but we will not allow our families to be subject to the dictation and whims of prison officers who are emotionally involved, understandable, but never nevertheless emotional. The prison officers cannot possibly justify their actions and the public will of course draw its own conclusion. It would be interesting if court proceedings were instituted by the prisoners to test the validity of the prison officers' action. We are always encouraged and exhorted to obey the law but what incentive do we get when there are two laws?

We have no ill will to prison officers and in fact quite a rapport has grown up over the years and it is our genuine wish that this good feeling continues but it is not being helped along by this recent episode.

We welcome the POA's announcement about concern for prisoners and their welfare and rehabilitation but we can assure them that the men of the UVF/RHC 'stationed' in Long Kesh Prison Camp are not in need of rehabilitation and we are more than capable of looking after our own welfare thank you very much. Nevertheless we are grateful for the offer and it shows that some prison officers do care.

In conclusion, we would ask the prison officers not to allow themselves to be used as a political instrument in the phasing out of political or special category status. It is alright for a politician to make an order in council deciding on such matters but it is quite another thing for the prison officers to try to implement such a disastrous decision. We were sad when we saw the prison officers dressed and arrayed in full riot gear ie helmets, shields, long batons, flak jackets (if you please), shin guards, and elbow pads at the time of their altercation with UDA prisoners in Long Kesh. They are not meant for this job and I am glad they have gone into print to this effect. We can take it then that we shall never see them dressed like this again and we shall not see the scenes we had witnessed on that occasion which we related to the Board of Inquiry set up to investigate allegations of brutality.

This letter was sent to the Belfast Headquarters to be released to the press. A further letter was sent to the POA which read:

Compound 21
Long Kesh Prison Camp

To Principle Officers
Larkin & Brown

9th October 1976

I have received an unofficial and unqualified report to the effect that all prison officers have refused, or have been instructed to refuse, to conduct my men of the UVF/RHC resident here in Long Kesh to and from the prison visits.

I have also gleaned that no letters will be permitted to my men by your men and newspapers have been discontinued to my men by your men. Parcels and handicrafts have also been arbitrarily stopped by your men.

In such a situation common courtesy demands that senior officials of the authorised establishment or representatives from the POA spell out the complete entailment of this arbitrary and purely illegal action by the prison officers. I am led to believe that internal communication and movement by prisoners is still in progress (doctors, medical treatment, and football, etc), as well as visits to solicitors and clergy, and I suspect court productions. If this is the case I can at the very least regret the decision by the POA because it appears to me the embargoes placed are highly selective and specifically designed to cause the utmost hardship to the dependants of UVF/RHC prisoners. You note we do not state UVF/RHC prisoners, because as soldiers part of our duty is to suffer and we responsibly and calmly take everything in our stride. However, that does not mean that we give cognisance to the actions of the prisoner officers or that we may not dispense with the services of the prison officers altogether. We have hitherto been uninvolved in any action or counteraction but I cannot allow prison officers or anyone else for that matter to take arbitrary and vindictive action against any of those men under my command without some form of redress.

We have a reputation second to none in this camp but it appears that it means nothing to you; we have often acted the role of peacemakers but it is manifestly clear that this has been taken as some kind of weakness. I can assure you that this would be a mistake.

I would welcome any information that you may give me in order to pacify my men and to attempt to give some rational explanation why the suppression is being brought to bear upon them.

The prison officers have always claimed that they are not politically involved yet such embargoes have the deepest of political connotations and indeed implications. However, I assume that you have a prepared course of action.

My men as a whole, and I personally, deeply regret and deplore the untimely and tragic death of Mr Hamilton from Londonderry and is his passing not a manifestation of the whole tragedy that has become a daily occurrence on the streets of Ulster.

These letters reflect the anger among prisoners that once again we were being punished for something that someone else was responsible. Not only were we being unjustly punished but our families were also on the receiving end of this collective punishment. The regime and POA were given till 1.00 pm to respond to our letter. The semaphorists were dispatched to the roofs of the hut and began sending messages to our other compounds in the camp. Prisoners in each compound were addressed by their relative OCs and made aware of the situation or as much of what they knew. Prisoners were growing angrier by the minute.

As the prison population grew so did the number of prison officers and now they carried a lot of weight and influence. Although there was a UK Prison Officers Association, 95 per cent of the Northern Ireland prisoner officers decided to form their own Northern Ireland Prison Officers Association. They were constantly locked in confrontation with the prison authorities rather than the prisoners and most of those confrontations were centred on money bonuses and perks such as shift payments, danger bonuses, incremental payments etc. However with the prison service to the fore in the dirty protest at the H Blocks, they had a lot of leverage to exercise when they chose to do so. We prisoners were often sandwiched in between those confrontations. Quite often the prison regime couldn't deliver a proper prison service because of the influence of the POA. Even the government on occasions had to succumb to their pressure.

As expected there was no response from the prison regime or the POA, the following communiqué was sent out ironically via a friendly prison officer whom we had used before for special situations. It read:

As a consequence of the prison officers' illegal action in stopping men's visits and food parcels we have decided upon the following;

Until prison officers fulfilled the services which they were supposed to we would withdraw all cooperation. This entails not permitting prison officers to enter any UVF/RHC compounds. Refusing to be locked up in huts and refusing to allow searches of the compound. The prison may attempt to take action against us either physically or disciplinary but we will resist both to effect. We are prepared to resist this unjust and illegal action and will not back away from it. If anything happens you will at least know the true situation and can act accordingly. We will not suggest anything to you and you must act as you see fit with an eye of course on public opinion. The dead officer is being buried on Monday and things should return to normal but knowing Long Kesh anything could happen.

We also transmitted coded messages to the outside from our new fangled Long Kesh radio confirming our latest position in regard to the prison officers and requested that radio contact be maintained '24/7'. We knew we were putting the radio in jeopardy of being discovered but such was the seriousness of the situation that we were prepared to lose it.

We then commandeered Compounds 18, 19 and 21 and evicted the prison officers from the compounds. We secured the gates entering each compound and selected ten men to act as on quarter guard duty throughout the night so that we would not be taken by surprise should the prison authorities attempt to regain control. We all slept with our clothes on and with our makeshift weapons. We had the experience of so many protests in the prison that we were all ready for anything that may occur. The quarter guard were to mount patrols throughout the night and report anything suspicious to their senior officers. The prison officers came up to the gates at 9.00 pm and requested to enter the compound to lock us up in our huts as per normal. They were politely told to go away. It was at this point that the situation was at its most dangerous because we were directly challenging the prison authority and the government, and they could have requested the army for assistance. We all knew that it was likely that things would turn physical and we would eventually become overpowered and brutalised but we felt strongly about the issue and would certainly give them a fight. We had improvised fire bombs and other surprises for them should they attack us.

That first night none of us slept properly, as we were expecting the prison authorities to use everything in their arsenal to attempt to regain control of the compounds. It was a long night and as the morning light shone through the windows of the hut, we went about our normal duties knowing that at any moment the riot squads could come bursting into the camp. Every hour on the hour we transmitted out codes to state that we were safe. Protests and pressure were applied on the outside by supporters, anxious that the prisoners would not be brutalised or killed in any heavy handed response by the prison authorities.

During this time, the authorities had a lot to think about. Should they wait until after RJ Hamilton's funeral on the Monday and negotiate a return to normality, or storm into our compounds, risking either the death of a prisoner or another prison officer? They also had to take into consideration our drill, discipline and record in previous battles with them.

The second day of the standoff could truly be called the 'longest day'. Although we tried to get on with things as normal as possible, we all knew the dangerous situation we were in and were convinced that every gate that was opened or the sound of any vehicle was the riot squads moving in. The semaphorists were on the roofs signalling but also keeping a look out for any abnormal movements in the camp. The prison officers would wheel the food trucks up to the perimeter of the compounds at meal times, but despite being hungry we doubled our guard in case they used this moment as a ruse to attack. When we were content there were no ambushes, we sent out squads to retrieve the trucks containing our meals. There was no contact with the prison authorities during this standoff, which lead to further tensions within and without the camp.

At 9.00 pm that night a senior prison officer, accompanied by the compound staff, approached the gates of compounds and requested entrance into the compounds to lock us up. All POWs of Compounds 18, 19, and 21 were lined up in columns of three and brought to attention. Not a word was spoken or a noise made as we defied the request with our discipline and our silence. After a few minutes the prison officers left. Every man was put on standby and the look outs were put on the roof of every hut and vantage point. However, there was no reaction from the prison service, so we relaxed slightly and tried to get on with whatever we thought would pass the night away. At midnight we listened to the news on the radio and the POA had released a statement. They stated that normal prison services would resume after the funeral of prisoner officer Roy Hamilton, which made us feel a lot better as we felt that it would counterproductive for them to send in the riot squads at this stage. However, we were not dropping our guard and the quarter guard was put on duty just as previous nights.

We woke up the next morning and the night shift guard was replaced by the daytime shift. To us there was no change until normal services were restored and cooperation between our officers and the prison authorities were resumed. The funeral of the officer was at 10.00 am so we assumed that services would return to normal after dinner. At 2.00 pm every POW stood in ranks of three as we waited on the response of the prison authorities. About five minutes later a prison van arrived at Compound 21 and two prison officers got out and called two prisoners for visits. The command was given to remove the barriers from the compound gates and the two prisoners were given permission to leave their ranks and go on their visits. We remained in our positions as the van left for the visiting area and another van entered into Phase 6, where our compounds were situated. It stopped at the gates of Compound 19, where another two prisoners were called for their visits and the same routine was followed. When the van left for the visiting area, the order was given for the men to stand down but the quarter guards remained on duty.

The OC of all UVF/RHC approached the gates of C21 and requested to meet with senior prison officers. A few minutes later two senior officers and an assistant governor arrived at C21. Senior UVF/RHC from C18 and C19 were summoned to the prisoners officers' hut outside C21 and a meeting took place. Obviously we were relieved to see that talks were happening and we mulled around in the vicinity of the area. The quarter guards and semaphorists remained on duty as the intensive negotiations continued. The meeting lasted about an hour and the prisoners' representatives emerged from the talks with assurances that full services would be restored and no disciplinary actions would be taken against any prisoner. The quarter guards were stood down and the prison staff were allowed into the compounds to check the numbers of prisoners and then to proceed with their prison duties as per normal. It was to us a victory at the time and a relief that no one had been killed or injured. We transmitted to the outside via Long Kesh Radio that things had returned to normal and returned the radio to its secret hiding place.

I remember asking our radio operator what message had he planned to send if the riot squads had been sent in, SOS? "No!" he replied. He told me that to avoid any mix up over codes he had agreed with the radio operator on the outside to play the 10CC hit 'Rubber Bullets'.

CHAPTER 28

Last Seminar in Long Kesh

Report on Seminar held in Compound 21
Long Kesh Prison Camp on
Monday and Tuesday 5th/6th September 1977

At the request of the Commanding Officer, AA Spence, the Compound CO asked volunteers to take part in a discussion on various matters relating to the Ulster Volunteer Force/Red Hand Commando in order that a paper is prepared in questionnaire form for the consideration of the Brigade Staff.

On Monday 5th September 1977 some 27 volunteers assembled in the study where they were addressed by the Commanding Officer. The short opening address by the CO dealt with the principles of democracy and policy making within the paramilitary organisations. Also dealt briefly with the rate of casualties (arrests) suffered by the UVF/RHC; the weaponry and resources of the UVF/RHC; the objects of constructive criticism; and a need for an abiding interest by prisoners in the good and welfare of the UVF/RHC.

The meeting was opened for debate and the first topic raised by the volunteers was that of politics. The volunteers wished to know if the UVF/RHC should act as a ginger-group within loyalist political circles so that they could influence policy. Others felt that perhaps the government would smash any attempt to 'go political'. The CO defined what exactly the term 'political involvement' meant and gave a short address of Unionism and social responsibility. After further discussion the meeting agreed that, as a pre-requisite to attaining respect and recognition within the community as a progressive and constructive patriotic body, the UVF/RHC should adopt a political stance. It was felt that this stance should be founded on a 'social conscience' and 'identification with the social problems of the ordinary people'. Several volunteers felt that the continuing violence was getting us nowhere and that political initiative was the only way forward. The meeting then posed the following questions to Brigade:

1) Do Brigade feel that the UVF/RHC should adopt a political philosophy?
2) Would Brigade agree that such a philosophy must be based on a "social conscience" whereby the organisations can become identified with the ordinary people and the social problems that beset them?
3) If so, do Brigade have any plans to formulate a political philosophy and to project the organisations as a political influence?
4) If not, can Brigade explain why they feel it would be wrong to adopt such a political philosophy?

The meeting then moved on to discuss the disunity within the Loyalist paramilitary camp. It was felt by many of those present that, even if the UVF/RHC could negotiate a ceasefire and a settlement with Republicans, it would be ineffective because such negotiations would not include the UDA and other paramilitaries. It was felt that some form of unity need be achieved so that the various paramilitaries could work towards a common goal. The following questions were then posed.

1) Do Brigade feel it imperative that there should be a 'unity of purpose' and 'a unity of policy' amongst the loyalist paramilitaries?
2) Would Brigade consider approaching the other paramilitaries with a view to setting up a joint study group to seek ways and means of bringing about such unity?

On Tuesday the second day of the seminar the commanding officer opened the discussions with an outline of the existing constitutions of the UVF/RHC which he said were inappropriate and required either radical changes or be scrapped in favour of a fresh one. He selected various paragraph and sub-sections at random and explained that they were ridiculous and inconsistent with true UVF/RHC policy. The meeting agreed that some debate must be given to forming a new Constitution and Policy Document. There was one question arising from the discussion:

1) Has Brigade any plans for drawing up a fresh Constitution complete with Rules and Regulations, Standing Orders and Policy Manifesto?

The next subject discussed was the Courts. Volunteers especially remand prisoners were asked to express their opinion of the courts and without exception it was felt that the Judicial System in Ulster at the moment was corrupt and unjust. Sentenced volunteers expressed nothing but contempt for the courts which they felt were manipulated by Politicians and which were a travesty of British Justice. The remand Prisoners felt great hostility towards the courts. Some felt that 'safe cases' should be fought. It was unanimous that brigade should issue a directive on the matter. Questions posed were:

1) Have Brigade any intention in formulating a constructive policy on Diplock Courts?
2) Do brigade think it right that UVF/RHC personnel should continue to give cognisance to a corrupt judiciary?
3) Has Brigade any plans to highlight the corruption of the Courts by way of effective and sound propaganda?
4) Does Brigade not feel that it is about time that the UVF/RHC dispense with solicitors and barristers who refuse to 'buck' the system and who are potentially encouraging men to plead guilty and 'do' deals? Is there any honour or principle in doing deals with a corrupt judiciary?
5) If Brigade does decide to order UVF/RHC personnel to 'refuse to recognise the Courts', will it ensure that the order is strictly enforced? Not only so, will Brigade also ensure that all personnel are aware of the reasons for the order?

The subject of Police Interrogation was raised and the meeting felt that it was imperative that all UVF/RHC personnel be thoroughly screened in interrogation methods. It is felt that a special team of officers be schooled in legal procedure, judges rules, interrogation methods etc, so that they in turn can pass on the information to the men at special lectures.

1) Has Brigade any plans afoot to counter police detection?
2) Has Brigade any plans afoot to counter police interrogation methods?
3) Has brigade any plans afoot to educate selected officers in legal procedures, criminal law, judges rules, police interrogation, rules of evidence etc?
4) Has Brigade any plans to set up special anti-interrogation schools and lectures?

5) Has brigade any plans to 'deal' with the more obnoxious members of the RUC detective force?

On the question of the 'H' Blocks, the meeting felt that some constructive plan be drawn up in conjunction with 'outside' and 'inside' for a massive campaign in support of those who are prepared to 'go on the blankets' for better conditions.

1) Has Brigade any intention of assisting the men in the 'H' Blocks to obtain better conditions?
2) Will Brigade ensure that the UVF/RHC to a man will back up with suitable action the efforts of the prisoners in their campaign for better conditions?
3) If we furnish Brigade with transcripts for a booklet and for pamphlets on prison conditions will they undertake to publish and circulate such booklets and pamphlets?

The seminar was adjourned until such times as a report on the two day discussions had been drawn up for ratification. The report was sent out to Brigade for a response.

CHAPTER 29

The Hidden Battalions

IN ANY CONFLICT while attention may be paid more to the fighters it is the logistics of a conflict that prove to be the most important, or as Churchill said, an army marches on its stomach. The demonstrations and protests to support those on the inside; safe houses to stash weapons and men on the run; look outs and intelligence gatherers; transport; and finance – all those things that support and maintain a war – had multiplied tenfold with the increase in the violence, deaths and imprisonment.

Gusty, who served in the Royal Ulster Rifles, knew that no army could operate without the logistical support. While in his few months of relative freedom he initiated the formation of a people's taxi service known as the North & West Belfast Taxi Association. Not only would it give the community a cheaper service to commute from the sprawling housing estates but it would also give financial and transport assistance to the prisoners. He had almost completed his task when he was re-arrested in the Glencairn Estate.

The imprisonment of a person affected the whole family: mothers, fathers, wives and children. They bore the brunt of protests during our incarceration and repeated the tiresome routine of going on a visit. Most prisoners were from Belfast, so visiting Crumlin Road was reasonably easy, but when prisoners were moved to Long Kesh, travelling became a nightmare. To assist with this, the first of two mini-buses was procured and a transport scheme was introduced, leaving every morning to ferry families to Long Kesh. The people's taxi service gave support when there were any shortfalls.

Going on a visit was an endurance test. Visitors would leave their homes about 8.00 am to catch the bus. The half hour journey to Long Kesh was made more difficult if there were young children but families, particularly the women, were the backbone of support, and their loyalty and determination went beyond the realms of courage. At first there were no facilities at the camp for visitors waiting and they queued up on the outside in all weather. This problem was alleviated by the Quakers organisation, not the prison authorities, who negotiated with the NIO to manage facilities for visitors. It was not unusual for visitors to wait 2–3 hours before being called for their visit, then they underwent a body search and boarded a van to be taken to the visiting area. Inside, the relevant prisoner would be taken in a van to the visiting area, also body searched and sometimes strip-searched. If you refused a request for a strip-search then you would be taken back to your compound and would lose your visit. Due to the chaos of Long Kesh, prisoners were often brought to the visits to wait maybe an hour before their visitors were processed, and vice versa. We hated the way our families were treated and the indignity of the procedure they had to go through just to see us for 30 minutes. In the beginning, prison officers would curtail visitors to the 30 minutes exactly, irrespective of the situation.

Our families and friends also became a crucial part of the communication between inside and outside, smuggling letters and communiqués, as well as other items. They took immense risk on occasions and they became a lifeline to our existence within the camp. Whenever we were protesting about anything, they would be the first in line to support our cause through demonstrations, lobbying or whatever we needed.

Then there was the personal side of the incarceration, including the financial burden placed on families. Mothers with young children felt it most, as many had lost their breadwinner to prison and there was little or no support from the Social or Welfare Departments of the government. Indeed I remember Gusty showing me a letter from the Department for Health & Social Services, informing his wife Louise that her state benefits were being reduced because he was in prison. The organisation and costs of running the war and looking after the casualties and prisoners became a huge task, as described by Sam 'BO' McClelland in a letter to Gusty, which was smuggled into the camp following Gusty's re-arrest. His recapture was a major setback for the UVF as a whole.

Dear Gusty,

This letter may be overdue, but that it is should not be construed as your being absent from my thoughts. Having experienced this period away from home myself, you will realise that especially at this time, many are the thoughts I have, many the wish I make, that things could be different for you and so many more of the men I am proud to call my friends. Recently I was speaking to 'The Red' and he told me he had spoken with you, though only for a few short minutes. It is good to see him in freedom, once again able to live as he chooses and not be governed by an unfair authority, as he was for very long. While it seems that many of my old friends are home on parole, I have only met actually one, and that one being young and a wearer of glasses. No doubt you will rezalise to whom I refer. (Excuse the spelling mistake, I know I made it, if that is an excuse.)

Up to the present time, your pet 'people's service' is still going along as well as can be expected under the circumstances. Everyone still seems pleased. Since you left and I was left without the benefit of your brain-power, I have been making all the decisions on my own. It has proved to be no mean task, but luckily and happily, up until now anyway, everything has gone all right. Certainly mistakes were made that probably would not have been made had you been here, but fortunately none that could not be rectified before serious damage was done.

As you know by now, East was a disaster. A fact for which I must bear responsibility, but I console myself with the knowledge that I gained a wealth of experience from all that occurred over in that area, populated with an abundance of what you once called 'super Loyalists'. I witnessed personally badge wearers refusing to co-operate, their voiced reason being that 'it is unfair competition'. Work that one out, I can't. However I withdrew as gracefully as I could, and immediately began investigating the chances of success in another area, which as you know, is now progressing satisfactorily for us. To enter into all the details would keep you reading for too long, so all I will do is ask that you refer to the figures involved, and you will see there is little room for complaint as yet. Certainly from my personal point, the odd need for complaint does arise. Up until now this has happened mainly through interference from those least qualified, to be taking action that I considered detrimental to all that has been established so far. Thankfully, so very thankfully, those who count listened to what I had to say, understood my point of view, and supported my decisions.

While this has been the case to date, it is always a daily dread, the wondering of who will do what next, without first telling me of their intentions. With so many men considering themselves to be what in actual fact they are not, I suppose the described state of affairs is to be expected. Perhaps so Gust? However, when events occur without my knowledge, I only refer to events associated with my end of things. I am not in a position to answer questions (or tell suitable lies) when I am approached by those whom the said mystery decision affects, usually the drivers. I have tried to stress my position recently and at the moment I am hopeful that the end of 'mystery decision making' has arrived, though no doubt time will tell. As I have tried to explain, hopefully adequately, it is not those who can make changes who have been the cause of anxiety, but those who think they are in a position to do so, they are the culprits who, through their feelings of self-importance, do, at times, make things sticky to say the least. The 'old school chum' act is a constant cause of my having to explain myself that I do not make the rules, I simply obey them, as all will have to, the rules being there solely for the well-being of the service, both public and drivers.

God knows, I am anything but intelligent, but I will try to do the best I can for all concerned, at all times. As you know, the OAP free travel scheme has been a boon for our old folk, it really has. Could you please advise me re: an old codger who is abusing the concession? He seems to spend his day travelling up and down the road for no other reason than to annoy the drivers. One driver had him six times before lunch-hour. I know he is abusing the thing but we do carry OAPs free, and at the outset we never stipulated anything about the number of free rides per day. Up to now I have been very skilful in avoiding the issue but sooner or later I won't be able to avoid it. So your advice would be welcome. It's comical you know, for the old boy knows the drivers hate the sight of him and he seems to enjoy that fact. Limit his travelling? Think of the bad publicity. We don't want that. How about buying him a car of his own? Then there's always the obvious. No! too severe Gusty. Anyway you work it out. I will appreciate it. I have asked for consideration re seeing you, but I realise the pressure on your visits, so I will remain patient and ready in case a sudden chance crops up unexpectedly.

Well, Gusty it is the wee small hours, and Betty has been calling me to bed, so I will close now. I must be on the road at 5.00 am to collect the early morning workers that go to Queens University first off, and then some more off to STC at Monkstown. They depend on me and I would hate to let them down. The workers of the Shankill I call them. All married women and all Loyalist to the backbone.

I will close by asking a favour as usual. If you can manage to fit in a letter I would really appreciate it and it is my hope that you will remember me should a visit be possible. God Bless, take care, and as forever, there will be absolutely no surrender to the enemies of Ulster.

As Ever

BO

The welfare sections within the RHC and the UVF were very active, organising fundraising events all over Northern Ireland, Scotland and England. Local musicians participated in many fundraisers and the general public supported the functions. We as prisoners were not found wanting either. We formed a handicraft co-operative on the inside and all prisoners were part of this enterprise. We received customer orders for leather wallets, purses and handbags etc, and then we would allocate prisoners a share of the work and they would do the necessary task. The completed goods were then sent out and sold to the customers. The money obtained would then be deposited into a general collective account in the prison which made us self sufficient within the camp. This venture proved very successful and if we needed new games, handicraft tools, foodstuffs, anything we could purchase then we were able to pay for it ourselves.

Gradually the logistical support from the 'Hidden Battalions' was established and capable of engaging in a protracted guerrilla campaign, becoming a vital artery in our armoury.

CHAPTER 30

Going Home

I REMEMBER THE 28 JULY 1977 vividly. A prison officer called my name out and took me to the camp reception. It was the day before my release to freedom after serving five years of a ten year sentence for attempted murder of a Catholic in 1972. As I have shown, we prisoners fought a daily battle with the prison authorities as they continuously attempted to criminalise us all and reinforce their ideology that we were nothing more than thugs. On the eve of my release, they were attempting their last insult. To redeem their Christian souls they would take each prisoner to a Nissen hut at reception and allow him to select a new outfit from a display of clothes. They could then send you out with a new outfit and a pat on the head. So I knew what to expect.

I accompanied the prison officer to the reception, navigating the numerous double gates and security checks on the journey from Compound 21 to the reception area. Finally we reached an inconspicuous Nissen hut no different from the many other huts in the camp. I was escorted in and shown row after row of coats, jackets, shirts, trousers and shoes. The only problem was the fashion dated back to the 30s and 40s.

I took my time studying each row, coat by coat, shirt by shirt, trousers by trousers until I came to the final row that contained shoes. I knew what I was going to do with them so I retraced my steps, picking a shirt, coat, trousers, and shoes to plan my final act of defiance. I'm sure the prison officer was bored to tears as he escorted me back to Compound 21 with my little brown paper bag of goodies. I entered the gates of our compound, where I knew I would undergo the traditional pre-release ceremony administered by fellow comrades.

I was only back in the compound a short time when six of the usual suspects marched in, grabbed me by the arms and shuttled me out of the hut to the nearby water tower, where I was summarily stripped to my underpants and tied to the tower. It was no use resisting, as it was all part of preparing for your release. The main body of the compound then arrived with their ice cold buckets of water, jam, toothpaste, dye and any other crude baptising liquid or material that they could anoint me with. After they had satiated their diet of fun they then left me there for about an hour before they untied me and handed me a towel so that I could have a nice warm shower and hopefully wash everything off.

The relief of the hot water from the shower was beautiful and I pondered over the fact that this was my last day in prison and the next day I would be released. I hadn't thought about it much but now it was suddenly dawning on me that for the past five years I had lived a prisoner of war life in a prisoner of war camp. I had seen many people come and go, I had experienced many things, and now I was about to leave that all behind and return to 'freedom'.

I slept like a log that night and didn't even think about what I was going to do when I got out. I awoke just like any other morning, went to the ablutions, had a wash and a shave. It was tradition to hand anything over to your comrades that you wouldn't need in civvy street, such as cigarettes and chocolate, which I did.

Everyone turned out at the gate to wish me well and I walked out shaking their hands and bidding them farewell. Ironically I had mixed feelings about being released and I filled up with emotion because part of me wanted to stay and continue the friendships and camaraderie. As I walked out the compound gates to the prison van that would take me to the reception, I looked back at them all and it was heart wrenching knowing that many of them had many more years behind the barbed wire of this concentration camp.

It was a sentimental journey as I sat in the prison van looking out as we passed the various compounds containing thousands of RHC, UVF, UDA, IRA, PIRA and IRSP (Irish Republican Socialist Party) prisoners. Hundreds of prison officers, armed soldiers in watch towers, the silvery sheen of Nissen huts, wire fences and coils of barbed razor wire had all been part of my environment since July 1972.

The van stopped and the prison officer opened the doors at reception. I disembarked and walked into the charade of preparation for release. I was searched for the last time, signed the relevant release papers and, clutching my precious little brown paper bag of outdated clothes, I took my final footsteps to freedom and found myself in the prison car park. I walked over to the Quakers' hut where Councillor Hugh Smyth and Loyalist Prisoner's Welfare spokesperson Jackie Hewitt were waiting for me. They had been visiting a Loyalist prisoner that morning and I had arranged to get a lift in their car back to the Shankill Road and home. After the customary handshakes and greetings, I asked Jackie for a loan of his cigarette lighter which he gave to me. I then walked across the car park, over to the gate where I had been released, and put the precious brown paper bag down and set it on fire. I walked back to Quakers' Hut and got into Jackie's car with a smile on my face.

CHAPTER 31

The Long Journey to Ceasefire

I ENTERED INTO freedom from prison but not freedom from war. The conflict had become structured, methodical and in the words of the British government there was an "acceptable level of violence". I got a job in the Harland and Wolff shipyard in 1978 and quickly became a shop steward in the Transport and General Workers Union, rising to Convenor and then a member of the General Executive and UK wide Power and Engineering Group. My socialist inclinations were espoused through those channels. I threw my energies into the fight for workers and better conditions. I enjoyed it immensely but in the back of mind I was always thinking about the missed opportunities in the past to bring about peace in Northern Ireland. I kept in touch with my roots, working tirelessly on the issues of human rights, miscarriages of justice and shoot to kill campaigns. The Loyalist community were always and still are bereft of a staunch voice when it comes to human rights issues.

The shipyard was going through a sell-off period in the mid-80s, which I as a trade unionist was opposed to. I led the campaign against the proposed management employee buy-out, as I knew it would mean the beginning of the end of jobs and the shipyard as we knew it. In 1988, the sale of the shipyard went through and a few months later, two weeks before Christmas 1988, I was dismissed from Harland and Wolff shipyard for trade union activities. The chances of me getting another job were slimmer than before. I was an ex-prisoner and now I was also black-listed from every engineering firm in the country because of my trade union activities.

I couldn't sit about idle, so I worked voluntarily on welfare issues, welfare advice, prison issues and human rights. Gusty Spence had created a community centre in the Shankill area where he worked voluntarily and he offered me an office space for which I was grateful. I looked forward to this work every day because I felt I was helping the most vulnerable of people and campaigning for justice for all. I was a lone voice within the wider Unionist community when it came to criticising the government on their human rights record and their policies in Northern Ireland. It was also good to be able to chat with Gusty daily, especially conversations and recollections about the prison.

Near the end of 1990 there was a flurry of activity within the Loyalist paramilitaries, as we knew that there was a growing desire amongst many people to bring the conflict to an end. The different Loyalist factions – RHC, UDA and UVF – became unified under the umbrella of the Combined Loyalist Military Command (CLMC). In January 1991 they publicly announced their existence in a statement to the press. As well as this combination, there was also a political unity when the Progressive Unionist Party (PUP) and Ulster Democratic Party (UDP) came together to drive a political agenda. The PUP had been re-organised with myself as Chairman and Prisons Spokesperson, Hugh Smyth as leader, David Ervine as political spokesperson, and Gusty Spence and Jim McDonald as executive members. The UDP consisted of Gary McMichael, Joe English and Ray Smallwoods as their main spokespersons. Our task was to explore the political options and give working class Loyalists a voice in the world of politics. Two members from the CLMC were appointed as a watching brief on the politico's and then reported back to CLMC. On other occasions joint meetings were arranged between the politicos and the CLMC.

The first task we saw as politicos was to get out of the trenches and meet the rest of society. We had been entrenched in 25 years of conflict and been removed from general society. We needed to rise above the parapets, get out there and start expressing our opinions, vision and give Loyalism a public face. We met with church leaders, trade union leaders, businessmen, and any other shade of our wider society. There were many meetings, many hours talking and many miles travelled. We opened up avenues of communication between the Irish Government and British Government as we strived to get our voice heard.

The first crucial test was fast approaching with the announcement that the Secretary of State, Peter Brooke, was to hold all party talks on the 30 April 1991. The politicos and the CLMC held a number of meetings to decide how to respond to this fresh initiative by the government. Although we would not be represented at the talks it was very important for us to respond in a positive way. On the 17 April the CLMC announced to the press that they would be calling a ceasefire on the 29 April in order to give the political parties the space to develop any possible political progress. The Brooke talks began on the 30 April and were dogged with walk outs and disagreement, and never really got off the ground. The talks collapsed on the 3 July and the CLMC ceasefire was ended on 4 July.

There was one breach of the ceasefire when a Sinn Féin councillor in Buncranna, in the Republic of Ireland was shot dead by the UDA. The UDA argued that the ceasefire only applied in the six counties of Northern Ireland. However the PIRA exploded a 600 lb bomb in the Protestant town of Donnacloney and also shot UDP member Cecil McKnight, which could only have been interpreted as an attempt to provoke a response from Loyalists, thereby collapsing their ceasefire. I looked at this period more positively despite the loss of life. The fact that the CLMC could call a ceasefire, deliver it and reject PIRA provocation was to me a step that could be worked on and a learning curve on the way to a permanent ceasefire. The CLMC were not happy with the response from the Unionist politicians to their ceasefire and stated then that never again would they speak on their behalf. In future the UDP and the PUP would have the authority to speak and negotiate for them. This was a major step in the CLMC thinking at the time and it gave us politicos the mandate and encouragement to push ahead and steer towards a permanent ceasefire and resolution to the conflict.

As Chairman of the PUP we had to set a strategy within our own constituency of RHC and UVF. We needed to ensure that as many people as possible were informed of progress. To this end we categorised three constituent groupings, the general Unionist population, the combatants and the prisoners. As prisoner spokesperson, I was visiting the command structure in the prison virtually once a week bringing the details of any movement. The prisoners themselves were very cooperative and gave us a mandate to "secure the security and status of Northern Ireland first and leave prisoner issues to the last".

On Wednesday 29 April 1992 the Brooke talks resumed and were now known as the Brooke/Mayhew talks, but they didn't invoke any response from the CLMC regarding a ceasefire. The talks stumbled from deadlock to suspension until they ended with no agreement in November 1992. To keep our three groupings informed we had been able to get access to the prison and meet with the whole of the UVF/RHC command structure on a regular basis. Meetings with combatants were held in various towns across the country and we attended conferences, did media spots more often and tried to get our message out to the wider Unionist community. We felt we were getting somewhere even though the violence was continuing on a regular basis.

Then the Shankill Road was visited by an awful tragedy in the shape an IRA bomb which killed nine civilians and the bomber. Over the next 18 days 26 people were killed as we lurched towards all out civil war. I thought then how were we going to maintain the political momentum in such a violent cauldron? After the funerals and when everyone stood back from the abyss, I was surprised to find that there was a bigger desire to continue the political dialogue and bring the conflict to an end as soon as possible. The Downing Street Declaration and the Hume-Adams talks had begun. If anything there was a greater emphasis to move towards ceasefires and political accommodation.

The CLMC and politicos had been working hard in the background to come up with a document that we could work from and use as the bottom line. We drafted a document with six principles which we all felt would enable a ceasefire to be put in place. These were:

1) There must be no diminution of Northern Irelands' position as an integral part of the United Kingdom whose paramount responsibility is the morale and physical well-being of all its citizens.

2) There must be no dilution of the democratic procedure through which the rights of self-determination of the people of Northern Ireland are guaranteed.

3) We defend the right of anyone or any group to seek constitutional change by democratic, legitimate and peaceful means.

4) We recognise and respect the rights and inspirations of all who abide by the Law regardless of religion, cultural, national or political inclinations.

5) We are dedicated to a written Bill of Rights for Northern Ireland wherein would be enshrined stringent safeguards for individuals, associations and minorities.

6) Structures should be devised whereby elected representatives, North and South, could work together, without interference in each other's internal affairs, for the economic betterment and the fostering of good neighbourly relations between both parts of Ireland.

These principles were the margins we could manoeuvre between and they gave us the impetus to present them in the various meetings that were engaged in at various levels.

As we moved into 1994, the atmosphere made me think that this could be the year that the elusive peace we so longed for and deserved could be achieved. There was also a caveat to the principles from the CLMC to the politicians to get it right this time because it could be years before this window of opportunity could be opened again. The IRA called their ceasefire on 31 August 1994. There was no rush by the CLMC to follow suit, however they did realise and accept that a Loyalist ceasefire was inevitable. The Provisional IRA had killed a number of Loyalists leading up their ceasefire, so the CMLC had now a period of time to settle unfinished business until they would call their ceasefire.

On Wednesday 12 October 1994 I sat in my office in the Woodvale Road Belfast. In the office were Gusty Spence, Joe English, Winston Rea and the leader of the UVF. We had been tasked to draw up the Ceasefire Declaration on behalf of the CLMC. After about six drafts we felt that we had the final document before us. Two of the leading reporters in the Northern Ireland conflict, Brian Rowan and Ivan Lyttle, were asked to meet us. Within 30 minutes they arrived at the office and were given a copy of the Ceasefire Declaration. They immediately contacted their head office and a holding statement was given to the effect that there would be a press conference at Fernhill House the next morning. I wanted to shout about it from the rooftops as I was so delighted that finally, within the next 24 hours, we would be announcing to our people and to the world that there would an end to the past 25 years of war. I was also given the honour and privilege of chairing the conference the next morning. I didn't sleep much that night as there was always the danger that everything would unravel at the last minute and we would lose this much sought after moment of history.

The next morning I drove up to Fernhill House in the Glencairn Estate area of Belfast. It was now a People's Museum but it held a huge historical value for the history of Northern Ireland Protestants. It was formerly the ancestral home of the Cunninghams, who were a prominent Unionist family in the early 1900s during the Home Rule Crisis. It was also the Headquarters of the West Belfast Volunteers, who drilled and prepared themselves against the threat of Home Rule and then eventually became part of the 36th Ulster Division and fought in the First Word War.

As I turned into the laneway leading up to the house, the car park had been invaded by almost every broadcasting company on the planet. The room was packed with the world's media as I took the chair with Gusty Spence, David Ervine, Gary McMichael, David Adams, Jim McDonald and John White. I opened the conference, set the rules and then you could hear a pin drop as Gusty masterfully delivered the ceasefire announcement.

Combined Loyalist Military Command

After receiving confirmation and guarantees in relation to Northern Ireland's constitutional position within the United Kingdom, as well as other assurances, the CLMC will universally cease all operational hostilities as from 12 midnight on Thursday the 13th October 1994.

The duration of this cease-fire will be completely dependent upon the continued cessation of all Nationalist/Republican violence.

In the genuine hope that this peace will be permanent, we take the opportunity to pay homage to all our Fighters, Commandos and Volunteers who have paid the supreme sacrifice. They did not die in vain. The UNION IS SAFE.

To our physically and mentally wounded who have served Ulster so unselfishly, we wish a speedy recovery and to the relatives of those men and women we pledge our continued moral and practical support.

To our Prisoners who have underwent so much deprivation and degradation with great courage and forbearance, we solemnly promise to leave no stone unturned to secure their freedom.

To our serving Officers, NCOs and men, we extend out eternal gratitude for their obedience to orders, for their ingenuity, resilience and good humour in the most trying of circumstances and for their courageous fortitude and unshakable faith over the long years of armed confrontation.

In all sincerity, we offer to the loved ones of all innocent victims over the past twenty five years, abject and true remorse. No amount of our words will compensate for the intolerable suffering they have undergone during the conflict.

Let us firmly resolve to respect our differing views of freedom, culture and aspiration and never again permit our political circumstances to degenerate into bloody warfare.

We are on the threshold of a new and exciting beginning with our battles in future being political battles, fought on the side of honesty, decency and democracy against the negativity of mistrust, misunderstanding and malevolence so that, together, we can bring forth a wholesome Society in which our Children, and their Children, will know the meaning of true PEACE.

[This final draft of the Combined Loyalist Military Command Ceasefire was finalised in this office on Wednesday 12th October 1994]

When he finished the media fell into a frenzy of questions, but to me and everyone at the table, we had reached the point of no return. Finally, we had delivered to our people and our children the possibility of an end to violence and the prospect of a future.

Last Word

EVEN WHEN THE Good Friday Agreement was signed we then had to sell it, not only to our own constituencies but to the rest of the country. The PUP had fewer resources than other parties which meant we were all out almost every night scouring the country in smoke filled rooms to garnish support for a YES Vote!

During this period I went to a downtown women's centre as part of a delegation to speak for the benefits of a Yes Vote and had the strangest and most humbling experience. The debate was to-ing and fro-ing between those for and those who had doubts but generally there was a feeling of hope in the room. One woman got up to speak. She was elderly but refined and spoke very eloquently. She was fully behind the agreement and by the time she had finished everyone was convinced by her presentation that the agreement was the best thing that had emerged in Northern Ireland for 30 years. I was completely entranced by her and I thought, as I looked at her face, that I could feel some connection. I hoped to have a chat with her after the meeting but things were buzzing and I had to leave to go to another meeting.

A few weeks later I met the women who had organised the meeting and I asked her who the lady was, did she know her? She said to me "Plum, that man that you shot all those years ago was her son." I was taken aback. She then said that the lady had expressed her joy that I had been so positive about the agreement and supported me in the work I was now doing. What can you say to that? Her face never haunted me, it humbled me. Her dignity and compassion was so elevated. She was someone's mother and my victim was somebody's son.

APPENDIX 1

UVF/RHC Standing Orders

The leadership on the outside and inside agreed a directive on how the UVF/RHC Compounds would be managed.

Camp Document

Reveille 0900 Hours prompt

Before 1000 hours all volunteers will ensure the cleanliness of the cubicles: floors brushed and mopped – litter bins and ashtrays emptied and cleaned – all areas dusted. Bed packs to be made as per regulations. Personal cleanliness will be observed, washed and shaved.

1000–1200 hours

> All personnel will be detailed to duties.

1200–1400 hours

> Dinner and rest period. All cooking and eating utensils must be cleaned before 1400 hours.

1400–1600 hours

> All personnel will be detailed to duties.

1600 hours

> Beds may be made down.

Volunteers in respective huts at 2100 hours prompt and will stand by their beds for 'head count'. Noise in huts kept at minimum.

2400 hours

> Lights out – No Talking

All lawful commands from Officers and NCOs will be obeyed without question or hesitation.

REQUESTS Governor, Doctor, Welfare. Permission must be given from the hut OC before names are entered into request book.[1]

CONTACT WITH PRISON STAFF must be done through Officers and NCOs.

STORES Post, Medical, Papers, etc etc collected by appointed storeman and distributed by Officers and NCOs.

ALL VOLUNTEERS will make every effort to obtain UVF/RHC uniform for muster parades, ie black polo-neck, black trousers, black boots or shoes, black jacket and black cap comforter.

MUSTER PARADE One per week minimum, to be followed by Barrack Room inspection. Standard will be maintained.

---

1 Previous to this, prisoners had to give their names to Prison Officers. This action removed more control from the prison authorities.

UVF/RHC Directive on Diplock or non-jury courts

Further directions outlining organisational policy in relation to the Diplock Courts.

Camp Document

Since the inception of the Diplock Courts and the abolition of trials by judge and jury in Northern Ireland for scheduled offences, the UVF/RHC have, on particular occasions, directed their imprisoned Volunteers to oppose this imposition by refusing to recognise its authority.

By refusing to recognise this type of court, we are making a manifest objection to the courts in this country denying us, as British citizens the right to trial by judge and jury. We are not satisfied that the Diplock Courts ensure that justice is exercised. On the contrary, we believe that politically motivated judges are convicting and sentencing many Loyalists who would not be found guilty had they been tried by a jury.

We feel there is no other method of protest that we, as prisoners, can effectively make. However, we do not intend to seek assistance in this issue from our comrades in freedom.

As from this date, all Red Hand Commando and Ulster Volunteer Force prisoners shall be directed to act as instructed when brought before the Diplock Courts.

The exact form of action we intend to put into operation will be displayed on a directive and placed on the notice board.

UVF/RHC Directive

A Directive to the effect that, as from this date, all Ulster Volunteer Force and Red Hand Commando Prisoners will obey the instruction laid down in this directive relating to Diplock Courts set up.

1. All PE and deposition paper shall be forwarded to the UVF/RHC hierarchy within Long Kesh for their perusal.

2. All cases will be investigated and it will be decided into which category each case will belong. The categories are:-

   a) Personnel who have no reasonable chance of being found not guilty. Such personnel will not enter a plea, instead, they shall refuse to recognise the court and will read a UVF/RHC drafted document from the dock (see Appendix).

   b) Personnel who have a reasonable chance of being found not guilty. Such personnel will not enter a plea, instead they shall refuse to recognise the court and will read a UVF/RHC drafted document from the dock (see Appendix).

   c) Personnel charged with murder whom it is construed by the CO have a glimmer of hope shall present a defence as instructed by the OC or Commanding Officer.

   d) Personnel who have no clear-cut category into which they belong. Such personnel will act as instructed after consultation with the OC or Commanding Officer.

If it is believed that it is unwise for anyone to refuse to recognise the court, for specific reasons, then due consideration shall be paid and the personnel concerned will be permitted an interview with the OC or Commanding Officer.

No UVF/RHC personnel shall be permitted to display dishonour or cowardice or to drag the name of the UVF/RHC into disrepute through the innuendos of duress or threat.

Appendix

Sample draft for UVF/RHC personnel refusing to recognise Diplock Courts.

   i) "As a volunteer of the UVF/RHC, I/We refuse to recognise this court because it denies British Citizens the right to trial by jury."

   ii) "I/We reserve the right to cross examine and to be given the opportunity to make a closing address."

If it is decided that a closing address is not desired, then each closing address will be composed on an individual basis, depending on the facts of each individual case.

Camp Council List of Grievances and Complaints

In September 1974, the Camp Council, representing all Loyalist and Republican prisoners (sentenced, remand, internees and detainees) drew up an agreed list of demands and presented it to the Prison Authorities and Government Ministers. This illustrates how well the various factions worked together on matters of mutual interest.

Camp Document

1) <u>Compassionate parole system</u> to be introduced wherein all prisoners have a minimum period of home leave following the death of a close relative (wife, mother, father, brother, sister, son, daughter, etc). Also that compassionate parole be allowed to persons with genuine domestic problems of an extenuating nature and for the serious illness of a close relative (same as above).

2) <u>Detention</u> That the time lag between the initial detention of a suspect and his appearance at the detention tribunal be effectively speeded up.

3) <u>End of collective punishment and block bans</u> in the Camp (with each compound standing on its own merits). For example, if one compound abuses a specific privilege it should not be removed from all compounds as a result. ie in the case of one man placing himself beyond prescribed rules of behaviour of either prison or organisation.

4) <u>Starting up of a Camp Committee</u> (Faction representatives plus Governor) to discuss and remedy contentious problems that may arise and to facilitate the smooth running of the Camp. Camp Committee to meet regularly (say once per month). Although the Camp Council was a fact of life they were not recognised officially.

5) <u>Two decision making Ministry Officials</u> to come into the camp to negotiate the areas of grievance.

6) <u>A negotiated Special Category rule book</u> to be introduced. At present there are no rules applicable to Special Category Prisoners.

7) <u>Inter-Compound visits</u> (between different compounds of the same faction) to be allowed to Faction Representatives in order to eradicate local compound's problems of the same faction as they arise.[1]

8) <u>Visits</u> to be changed to comply with Stan Orme's statement in the House of Commons. This has not been done.[2]

10) <u>Improved conditions</u> for visitors in waiting rooms.

11) <u>Speeding up of visiting system</u> (this would follow if our proposals are put into effect).

12) <u>Star and Ordinary classifications</u> of Special Category prisoners to be abolished. This classification is inapplicable in this situation.[3]

13) <u>Vocational training</u> to be introduced.

14) <u>A laundry system</u> to be introduced that shall be seen as effective.

15) <u>Severe restrictions</u> on handicraft tools and materials to be eased.

16) <u>Restrictions</u> to be lifted on political literature coming into the Camp.

17) <u>Restrictions</u> on black clothing, towels, gloves, etc to be lifted.

18) <u>Food</u> shortage problem to be remedied.

19) <u>There is no delegation of authority</u> from Governor right down the line, making requests and complaints system a farce.

20) <u>Speeding up</u> of remand process. At present it is de-facto imprisonment.

21) <u>Improved educational facilities</u> Cassettes, projector, etc to be allowed.

22) <u>Education and lecturers</u> to be provided for remand prisoners.

---

1 This demand was the catalyst in the burning of the camp a month later. There are suspicions that Republicans deliberately forced the issue when a squad of masked Republicans attacked two prison officers in Compound 13. Prison authorities demanded Republicans hand over the attackers or they would send in the army to restore order. David Morely, who was the Commanding Officer of Republican prisoners and who was in Compound 16, requested to visit Compound 13 to deal with the incident. This was refused and the Army riot squads were sent in.

2 Mr Stan Orme (Government Minister) had stated that a more humanitarian approach should be adopted in the Long Kesh visiting issue.

3 Star prisoners are those who have not been in prison previously. Ordinary category is given to those with prior prison sentences. Under old criminal rules there were different rules and additional privileges for Star prisoners.

23) <u>Organised recreation</u> for remand prisoners to be introduced (eg use of camp football area).

24) <u>Dental services</u> for remand prisoners to be introduced. At present there is no service.

25) <u>End the practice</u> of moving men to Magilligan Camp against their will.

26) <u>Increase amount of money</u> prisoners are allowed to spend in camp shop. At present it is still 50 pence per man even though prices have spiralled.

27) <u>Disinterest of staff</u> They are only here in three month stints from English and Scottish prisons.

28) <u>Abnormal lengths</u> of time waiting on dental and optical treatment to be resolved.

29) <u>Introduction</u> of evening football or use of both pitches simultaneously.

30) <u>Flooding</u> in compounds and general lack of maintenance to compounds is being ignored by authorities.

31) <u>Remands</u> are left with a legacy of destroyed property from previous occupants of compounds.

32) <u>Prison hospital</u> is regarded as 'punishment'. There is a virtual 24 hour lock up and no television, hot water facilities, etc.

33) <u>Introduction</u> of prison films once per week. Governor's funds should be able to cope with expense.

APPENDIX 4

Account of UVF/RHC Court Martial

An agreed formula was endorsed by both the leadership inside and outside the Camp as to who could or could not enter into the compounds.

Compound 21

On April 1976 in the above compound, a Court Martial was convened consisting of the below mentioned personnel, in connection with the arrest, conviction and sentencing by the Courts of Volunteer X.

The facts surrounding the Court Martial arose of the above person engaging himself, without orders or approval from UVF Officers or NCOs, in a <u>self-gain</u> armed robbery of a small Grocer's shop in Belfast. In the course of the robbery, several ordinary customers had their wallets removed, thus highlighting the clearly <u>criminal</u> nature of this act.

In the courts, the accused was sentenced to 8 years imprisonment, and it was noted that his arrest and subsequent conviction arose entirely due to a statement of admission being made to the Police by the accused.

Signed: _____ Officer Commanding

Signed: _____ Second in Command

Signed: _____ Adjutant

The Volunteer was found guilty and was consequently rejected from the UVF compound as his punishment.

APPENDIX 5

UVF/RHC Directive on Prison Authorities

There was a constant struggle for control between the prisoners and the prison authorities.

Directive: To all compounds
This Directive shall be displayed on each hut notice board.
23 November 1976

1) As from the above date, no officer, NCO or Volunteer shall cause any breach of UVF/RHC regulations in this Camp that would render him outside the control of the UVF/RHC at any time.

   Any UVF/RHC personnel who is, for whatever reason, removed from the jurisdiction of UVF/RHC control, by being taken to the punishment cells or wherever, shall on return to the compound be charged with a UVF/RHC offence and be liable to face severe disciplinary action.[1]

2) As from the above date, no UVF/RHC will give credence or recognition or acknowledgement to any charge levelled against him by any Prison Authorities. All UVF/RHC personnel charged with offences under Prison Rules or regulations shall answer in the following manner:-

   "As a volunteer in the UVF/RHC and as a prisoner of war in this camp, I refuse to recognise this court."

   Nothing further than this shall be said and under no circumstances shall any UVF/RHC personnel sign any document put before him. Failure to comply with this Directive shall render the Volunteer liable to serious disciplinary charges.

   Commanding Officer

---

1 This rule was inserted mostly to prevent agents or police informers operating within the compounds.

Index